AF378248

SUSPENDED TIME

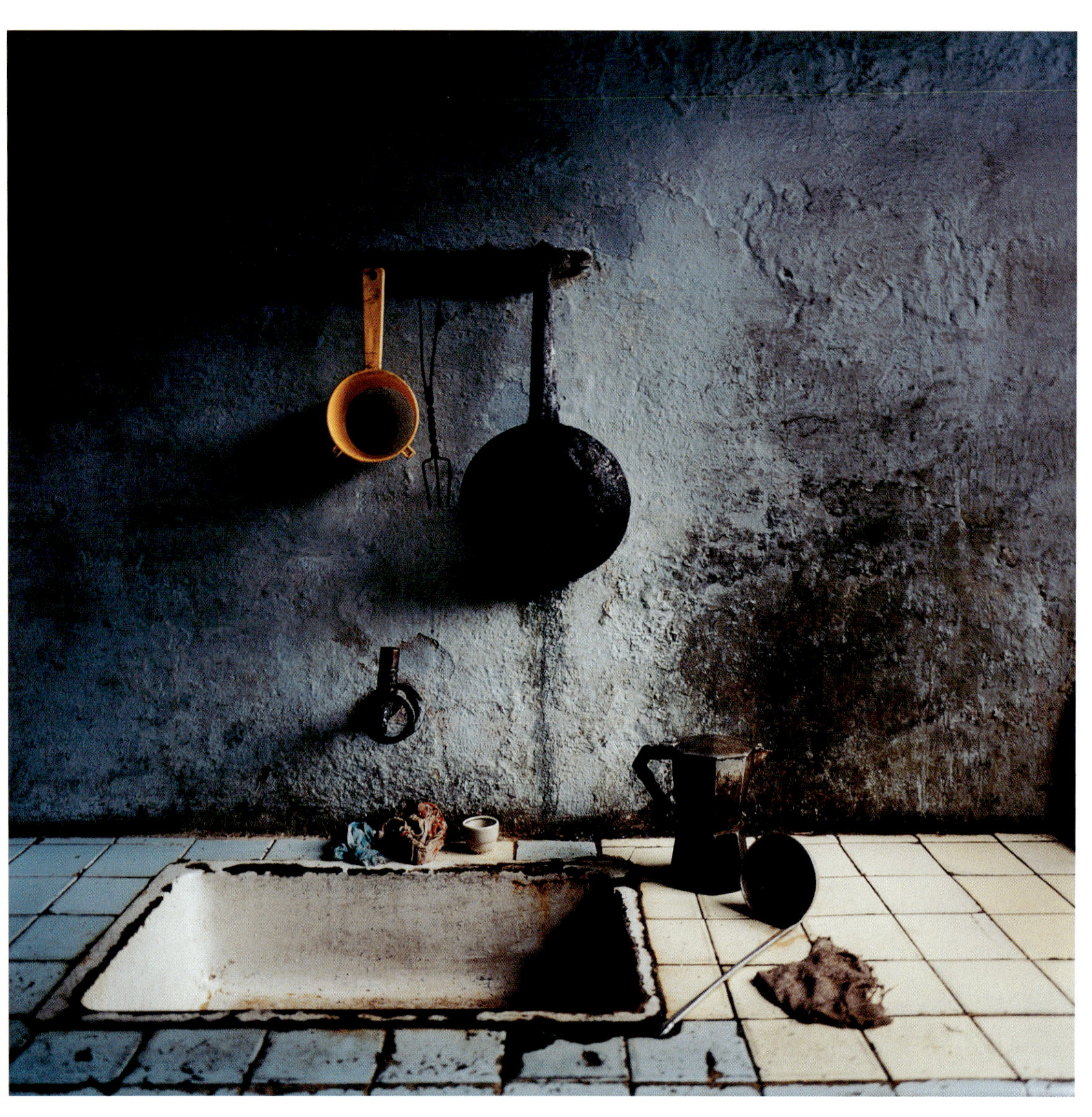

HARIS KAKAROUHAS

SUSPENDED TIME
A CUBAN PORTRAIT

Text by Ian Jeffrey

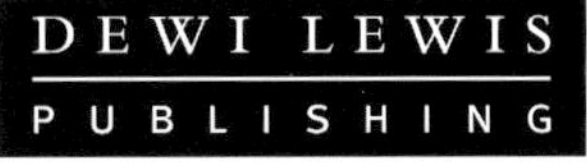

Special thanks to:
Rogelia Concebo
Mark Durden
Manolis Giakoumakis
Niuvis and Yoel Gómez
John Goto
Evi Karabatsou
Evi Karagianidi
Antonis Katsouris
Rene Lescay
Christos Logothetis
Fouli Popoli
Stelios Ramfos
Platon Rivellis
Oded Simson
Aris Skarpas
Katerina Sperentzou
Eleni Vambouli
Dimitris Vasilopoulos

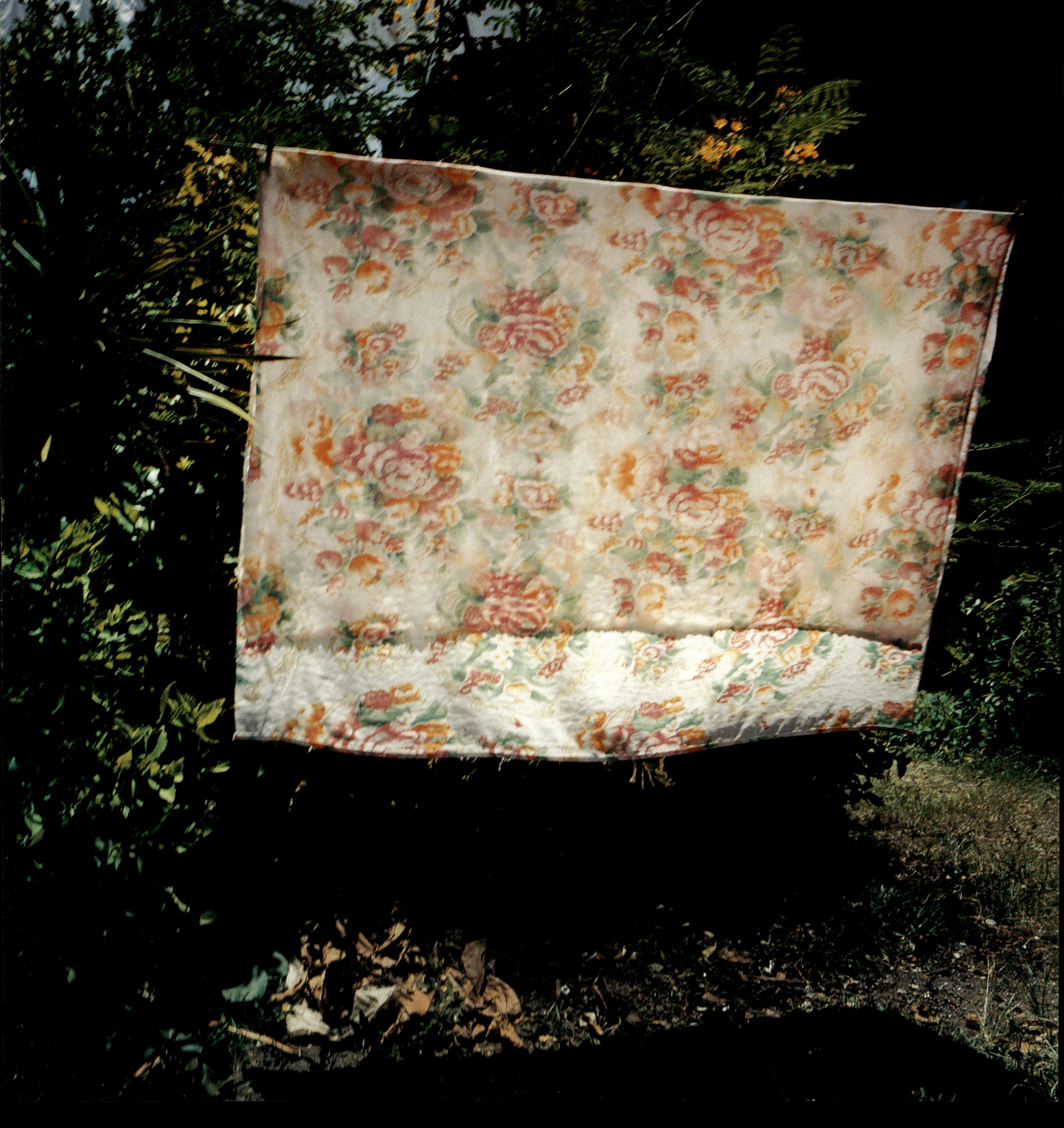

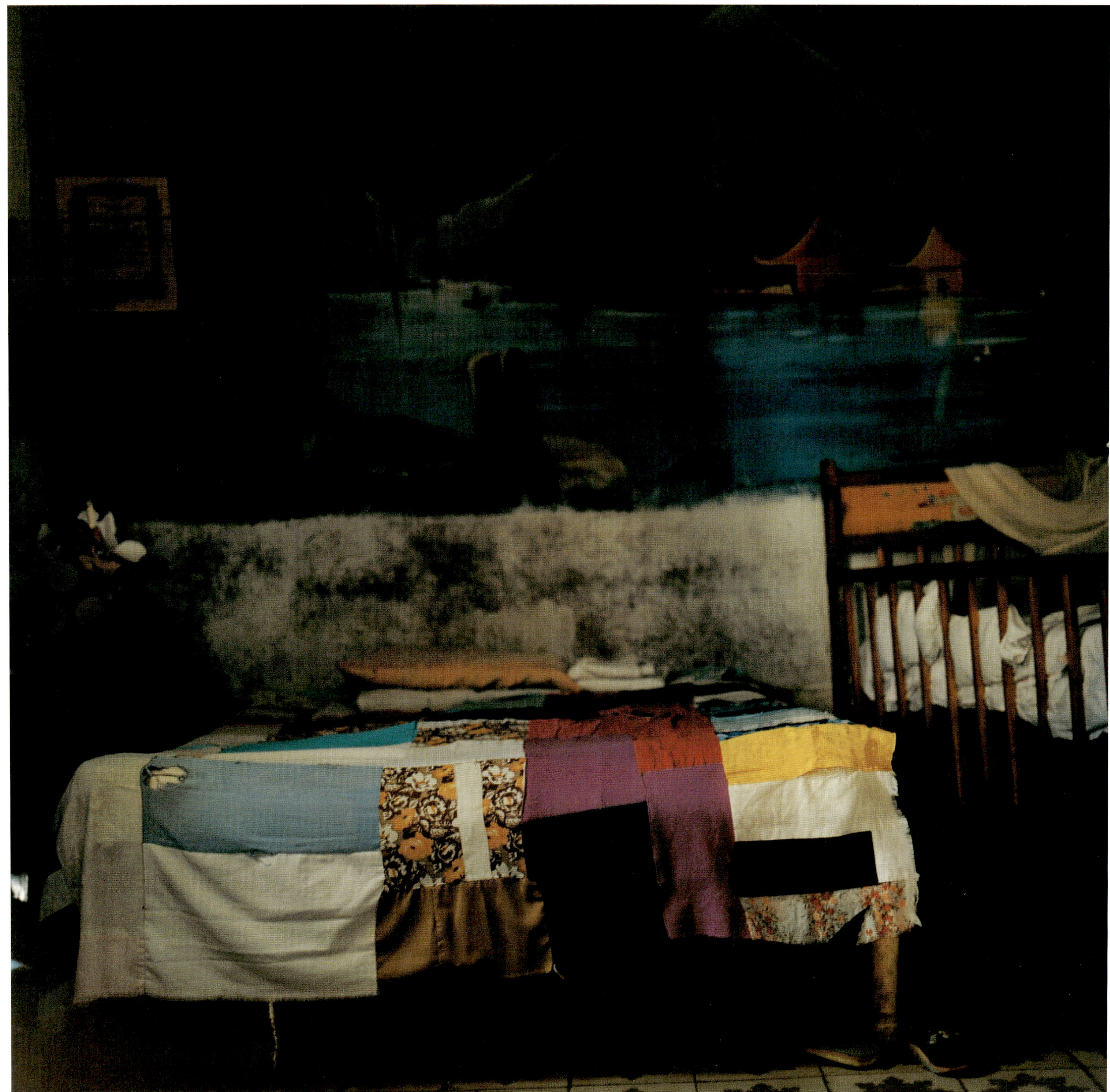

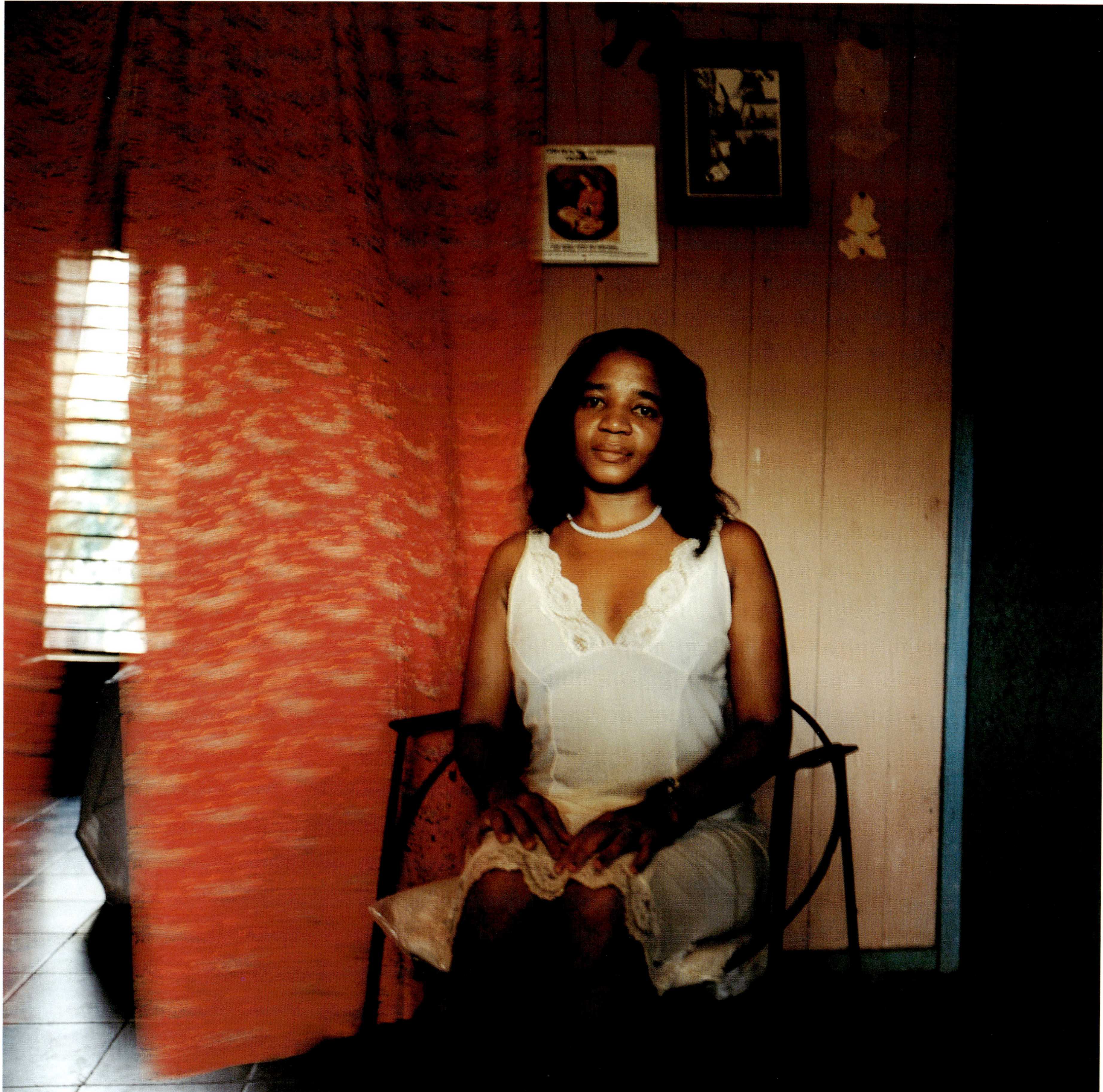

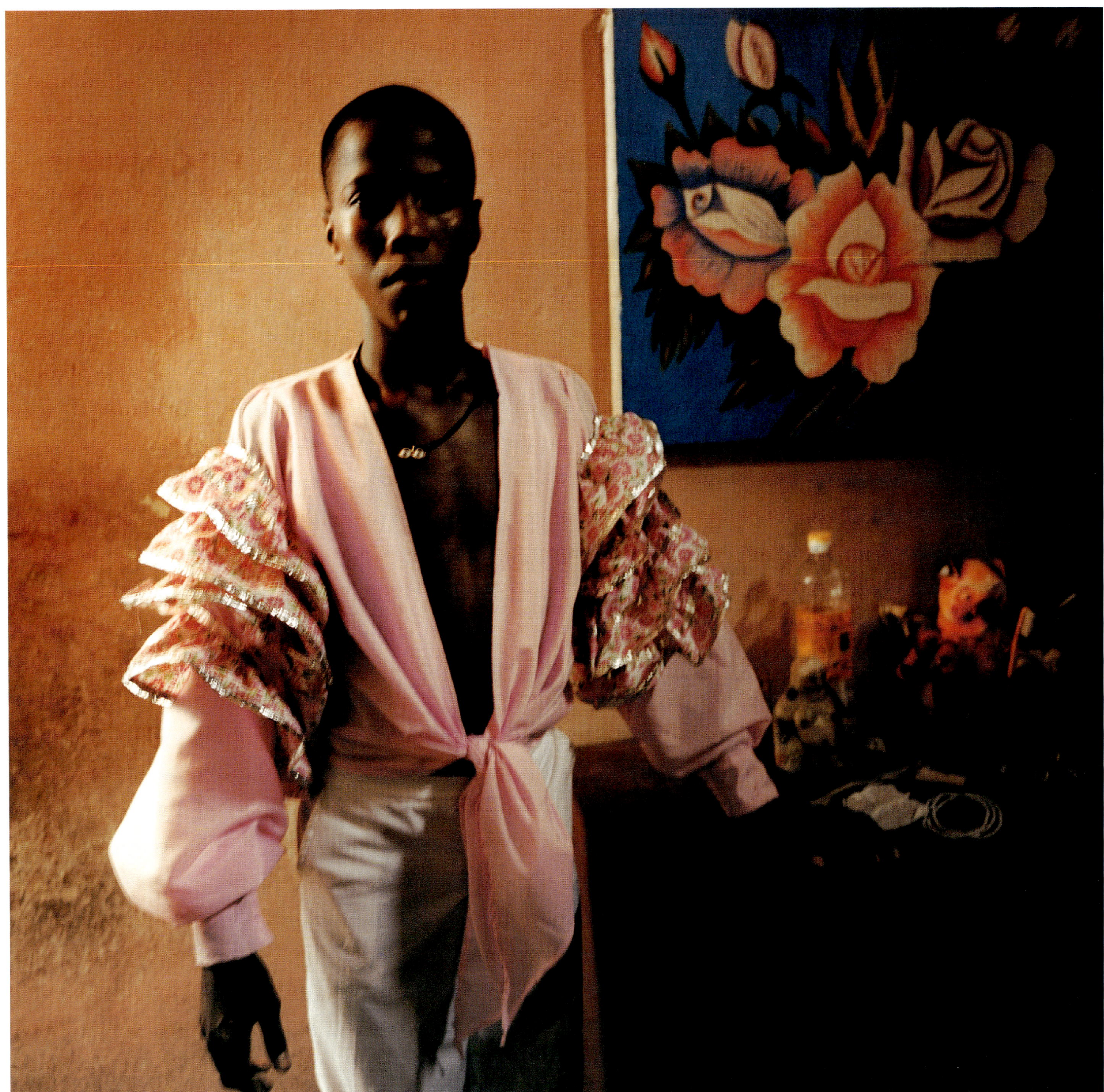

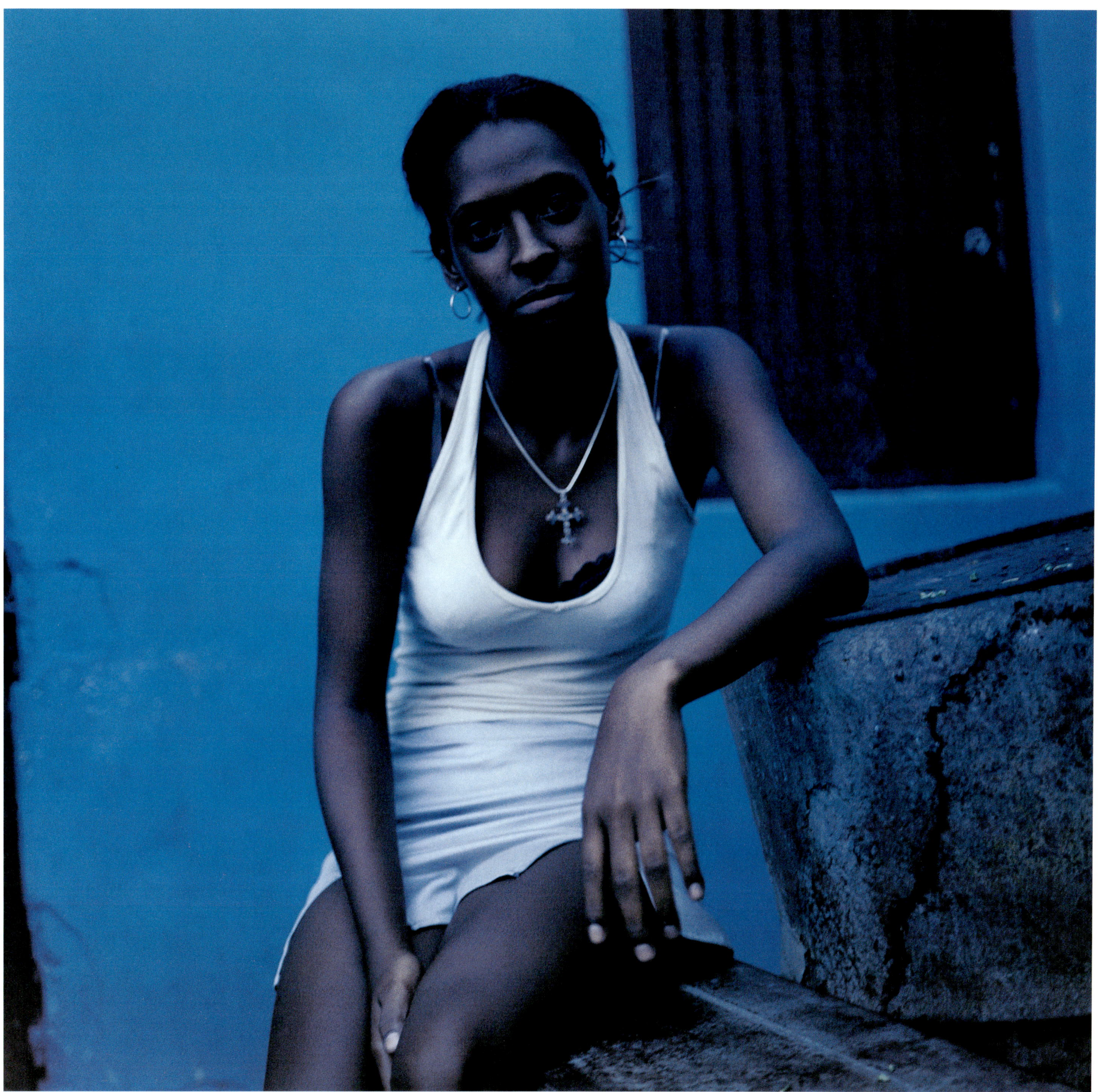

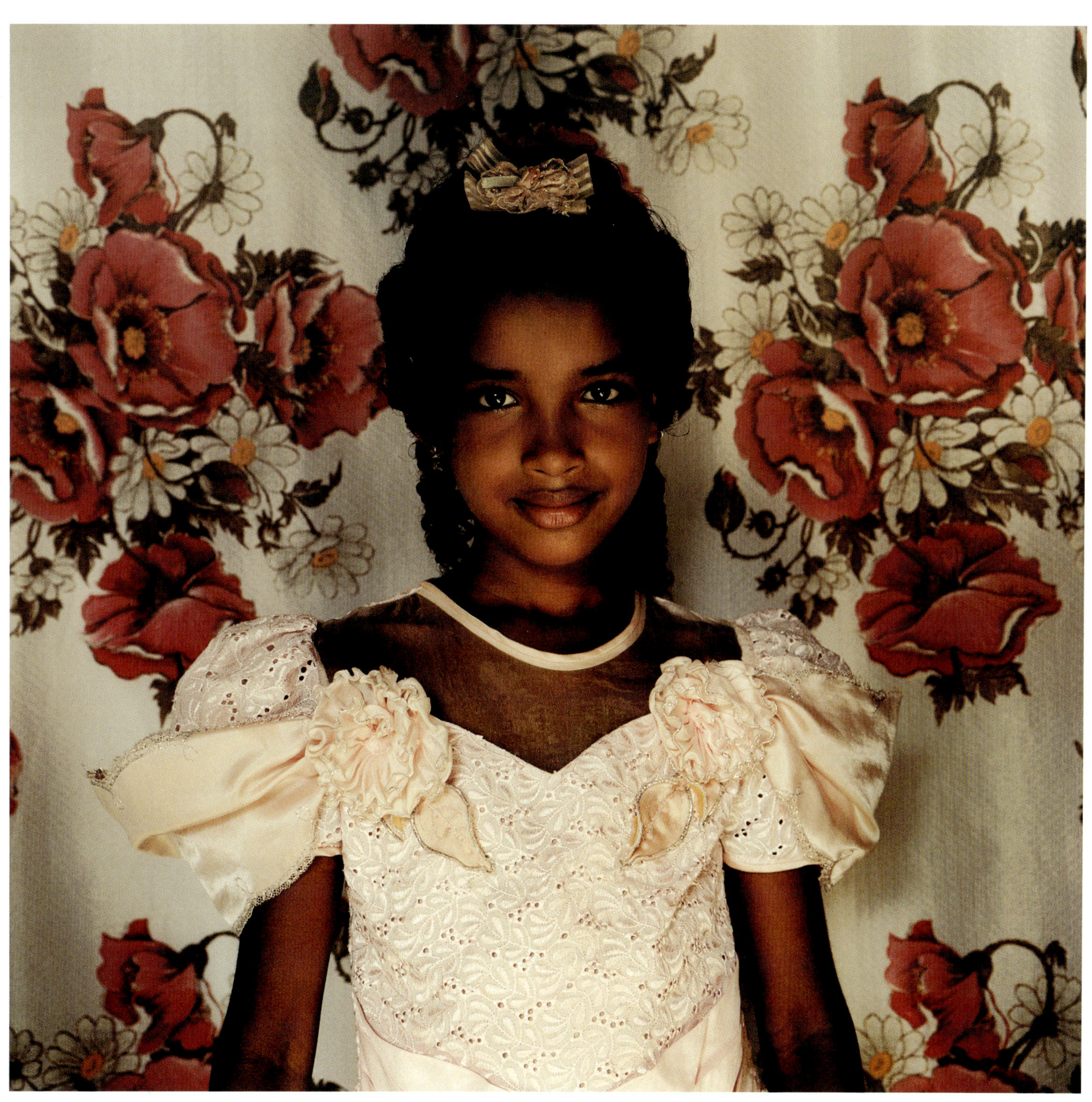

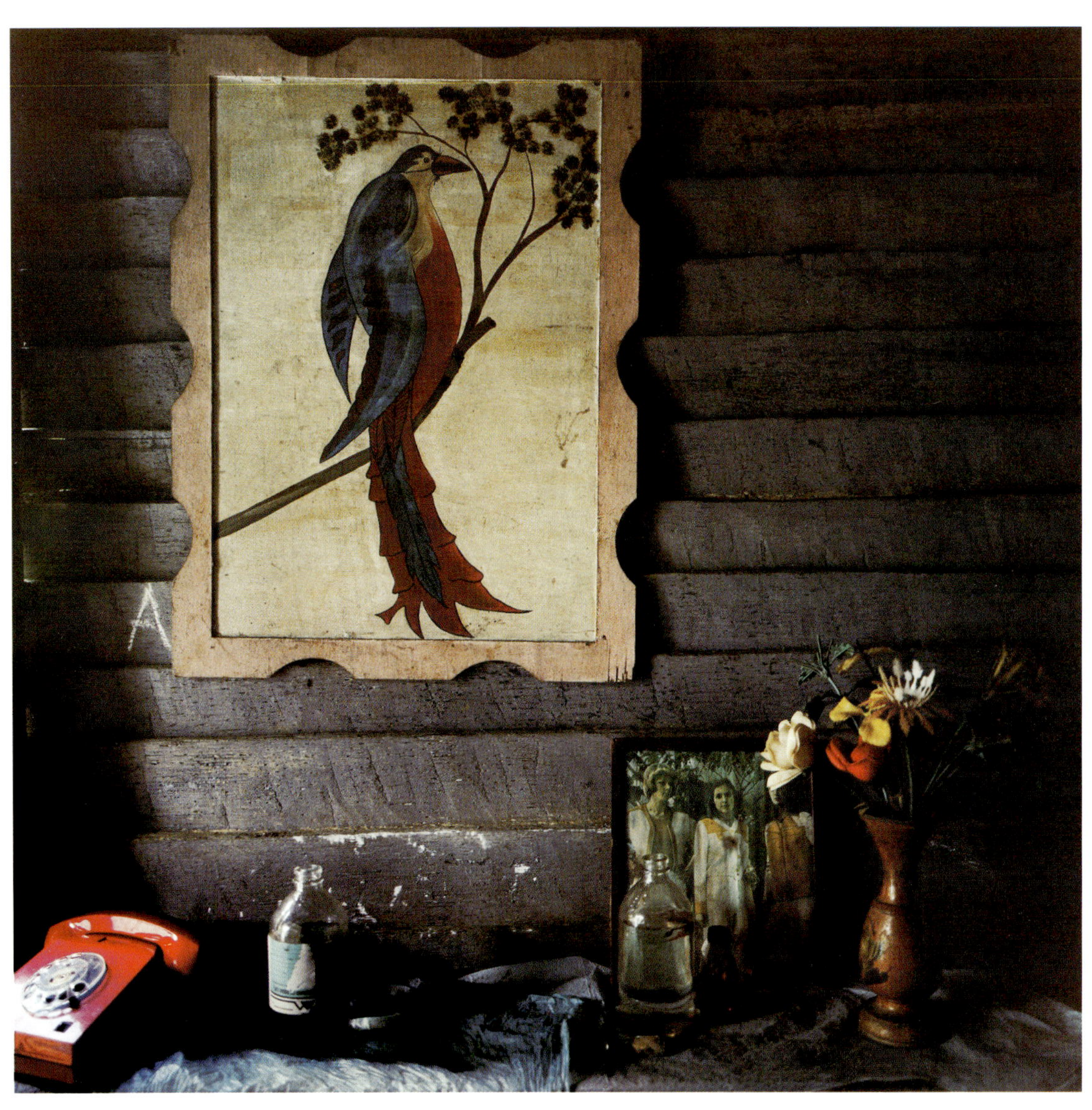

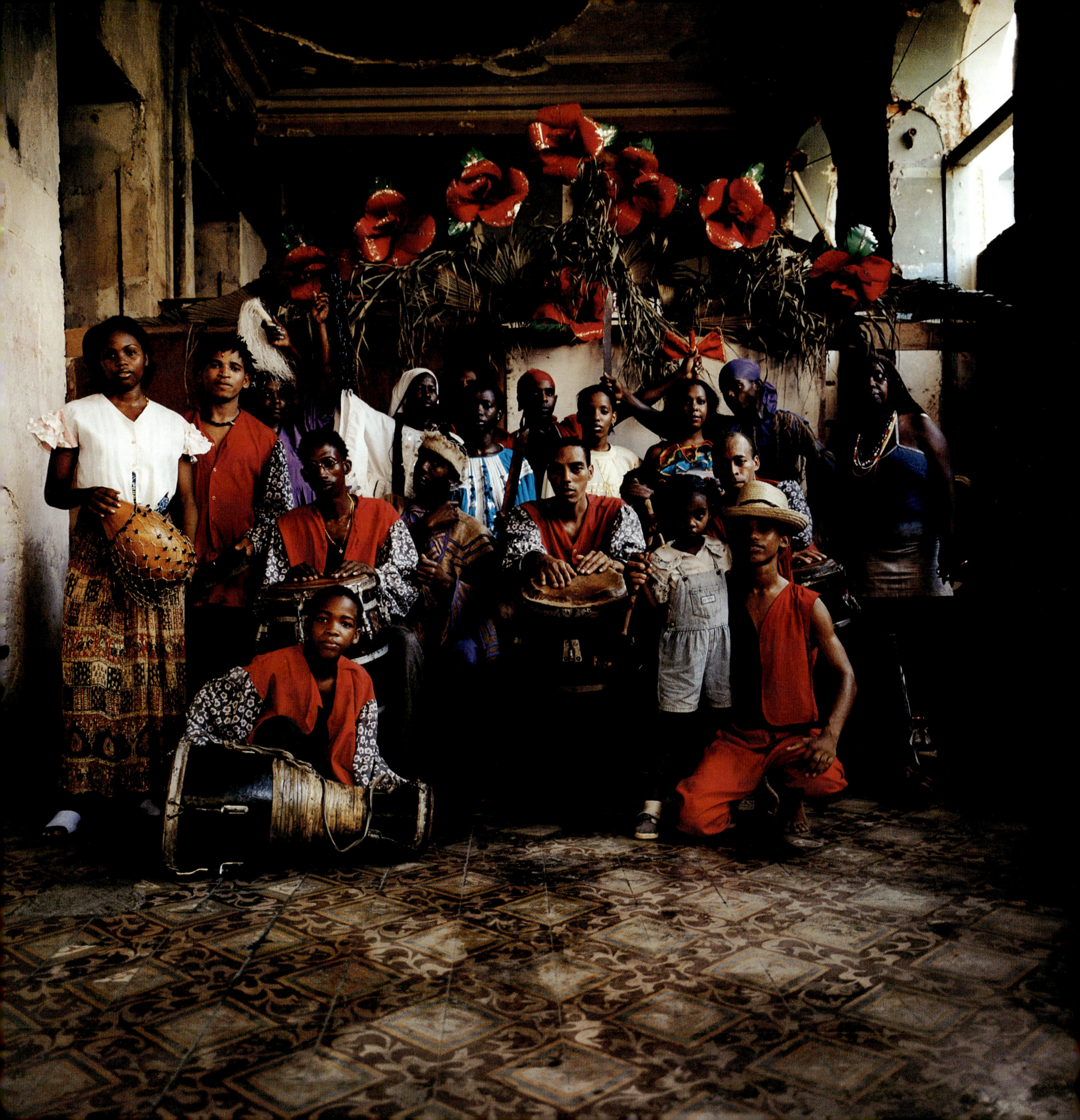

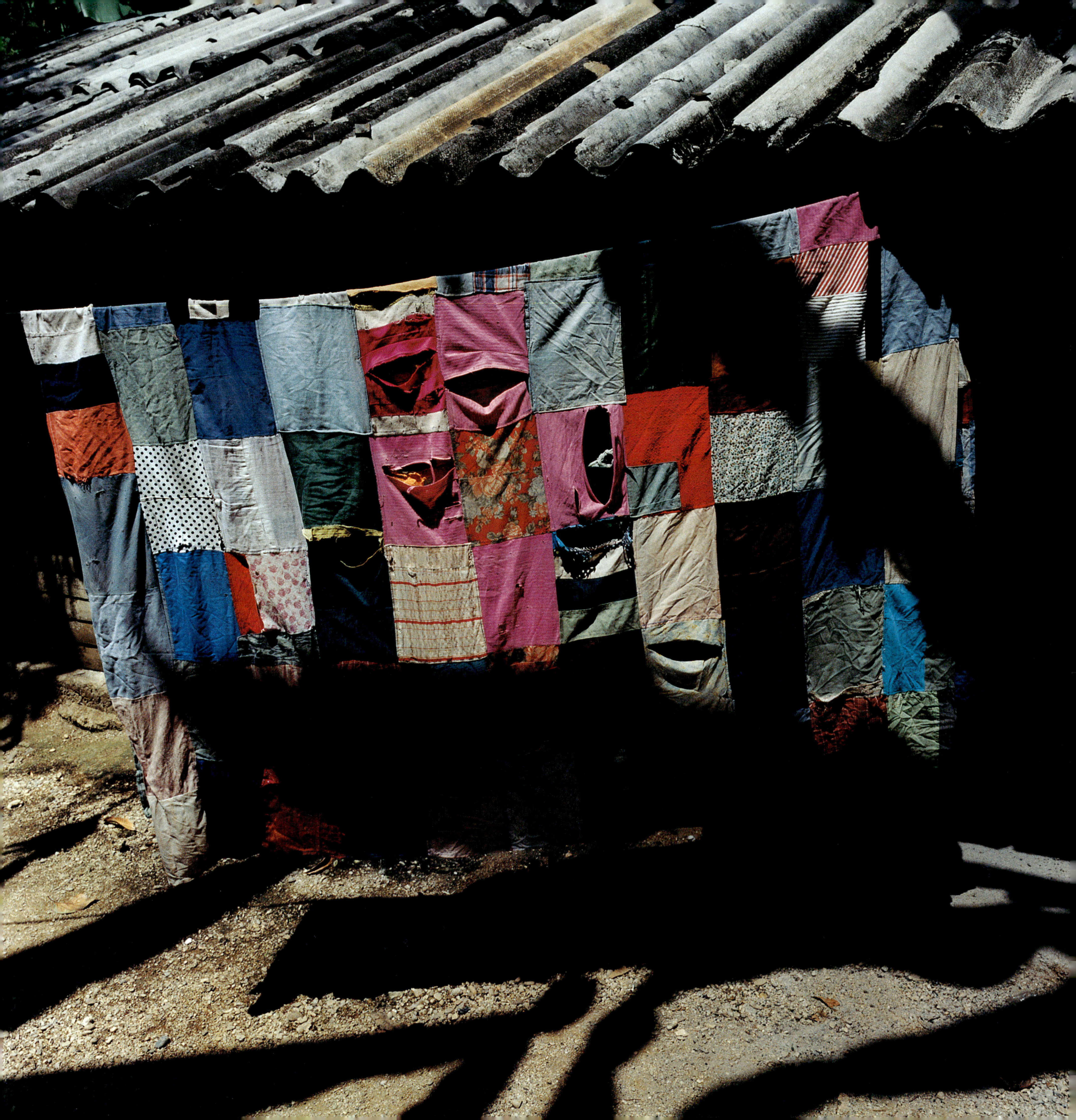

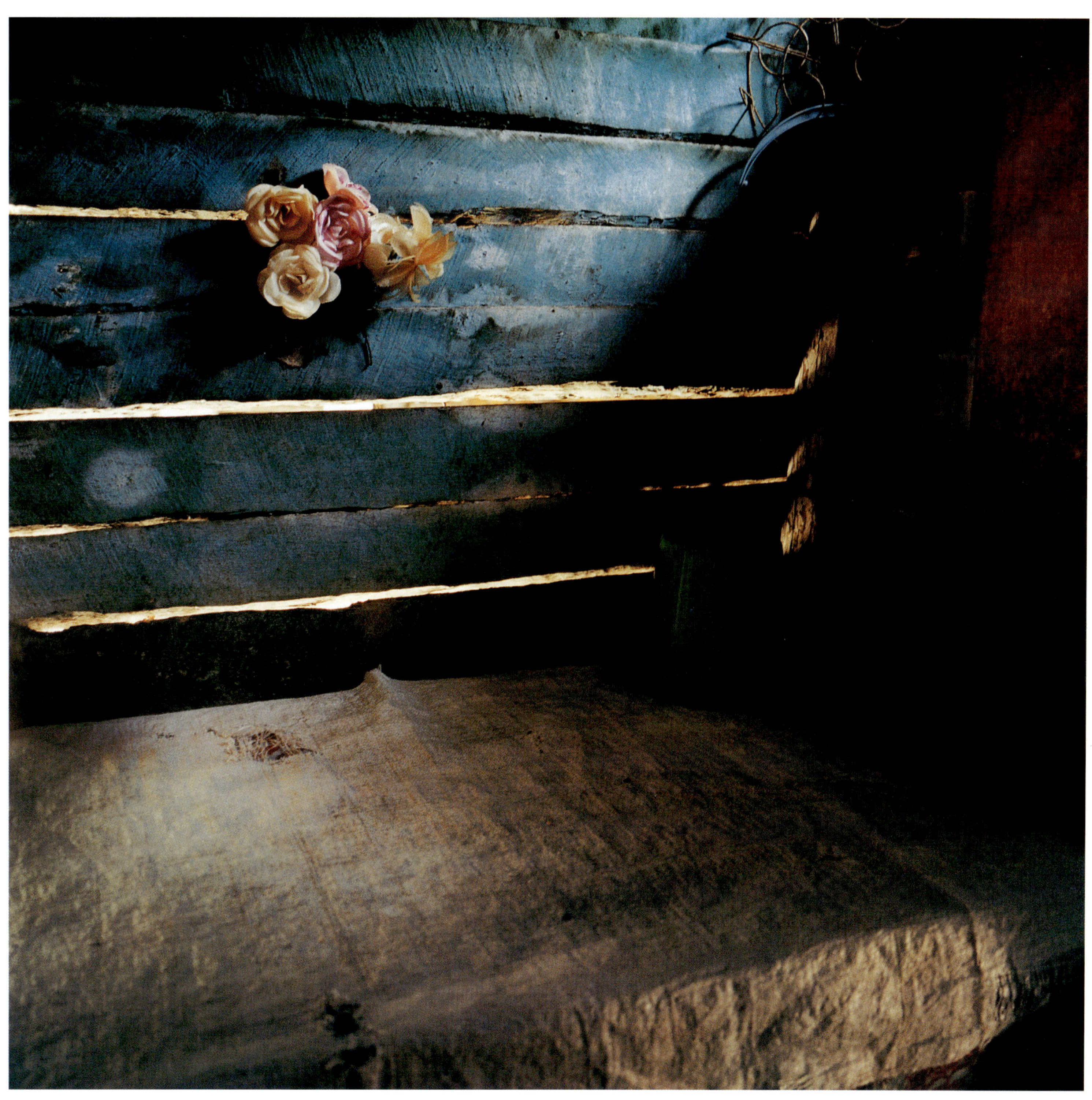

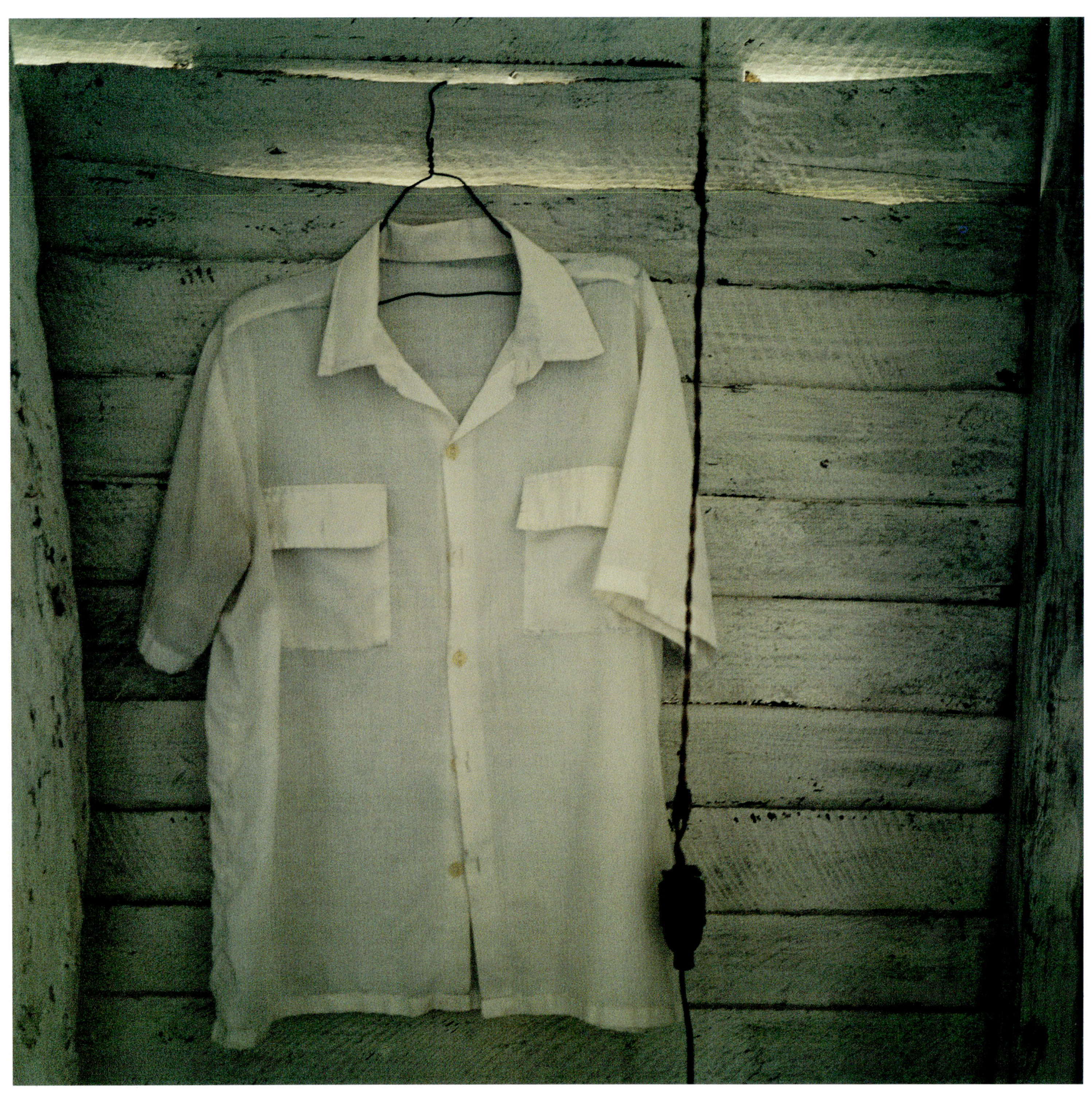

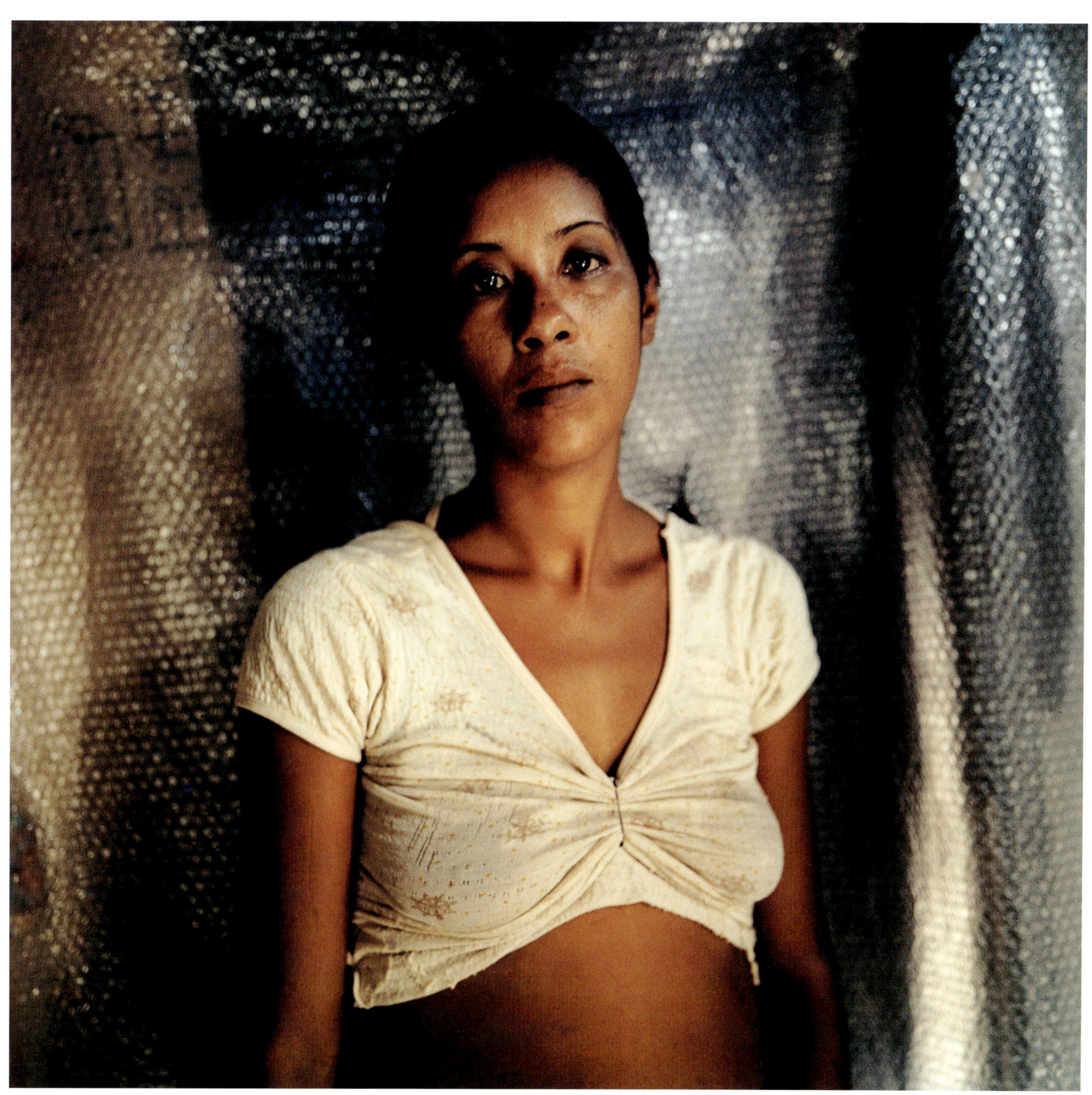

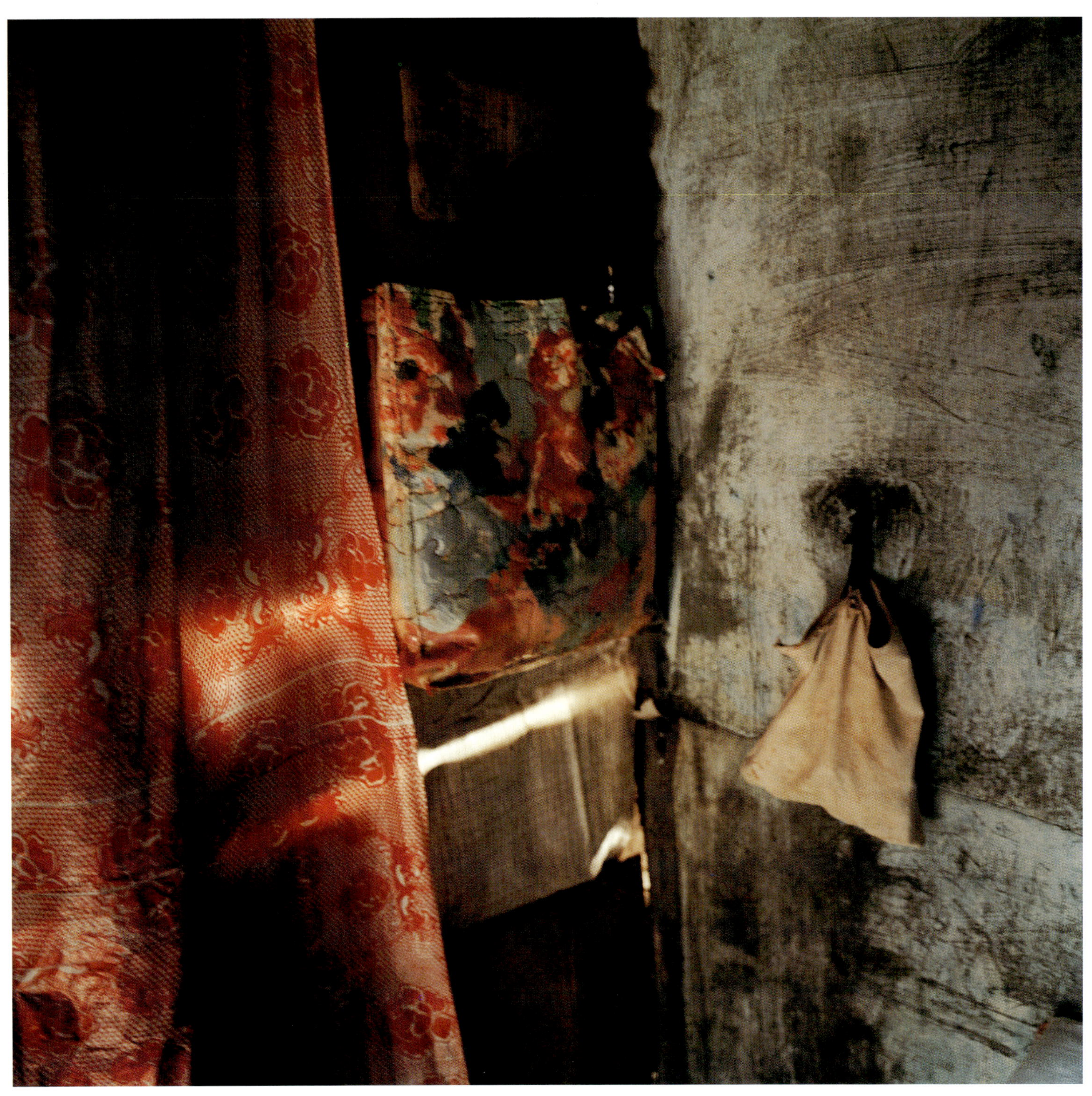

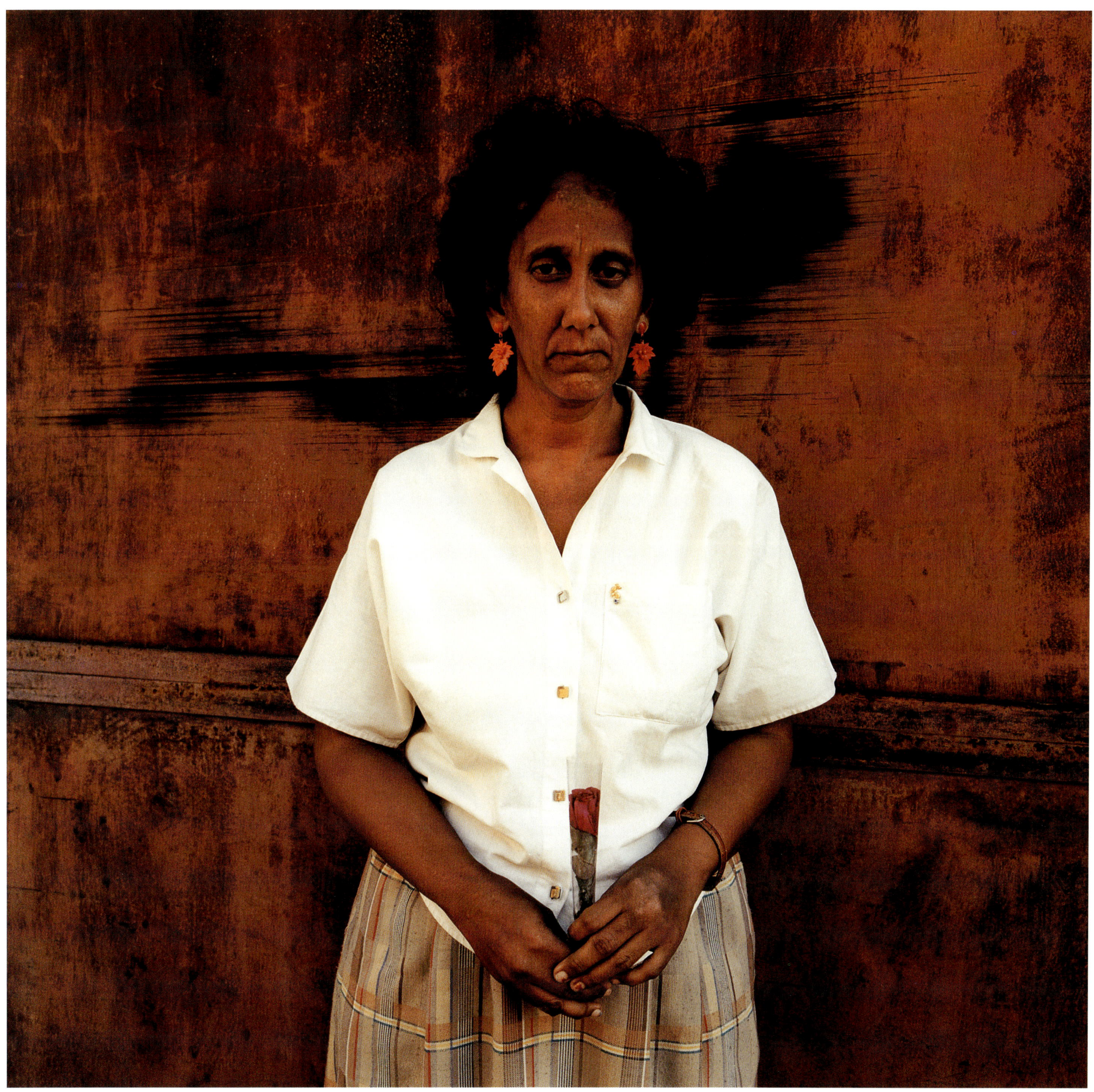

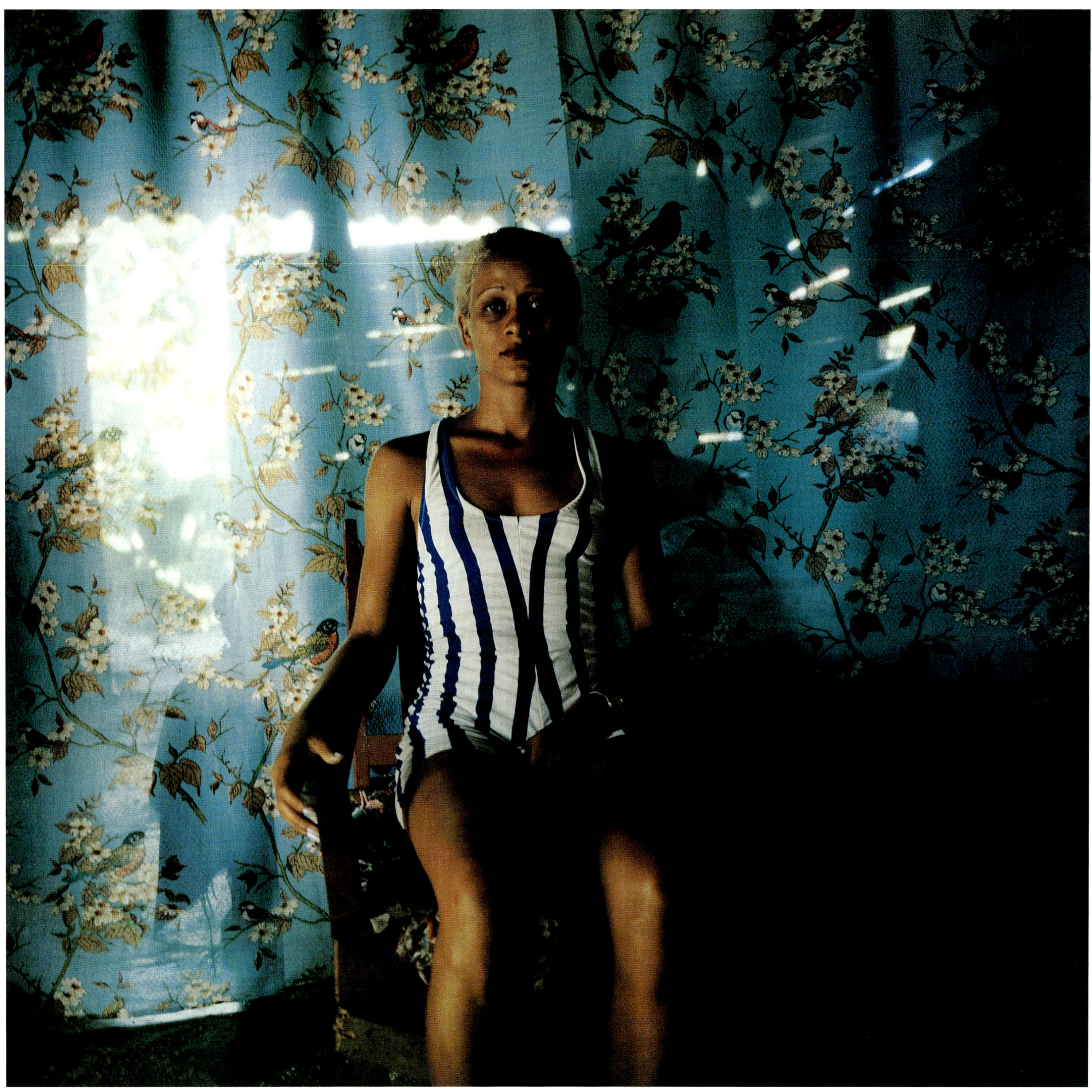

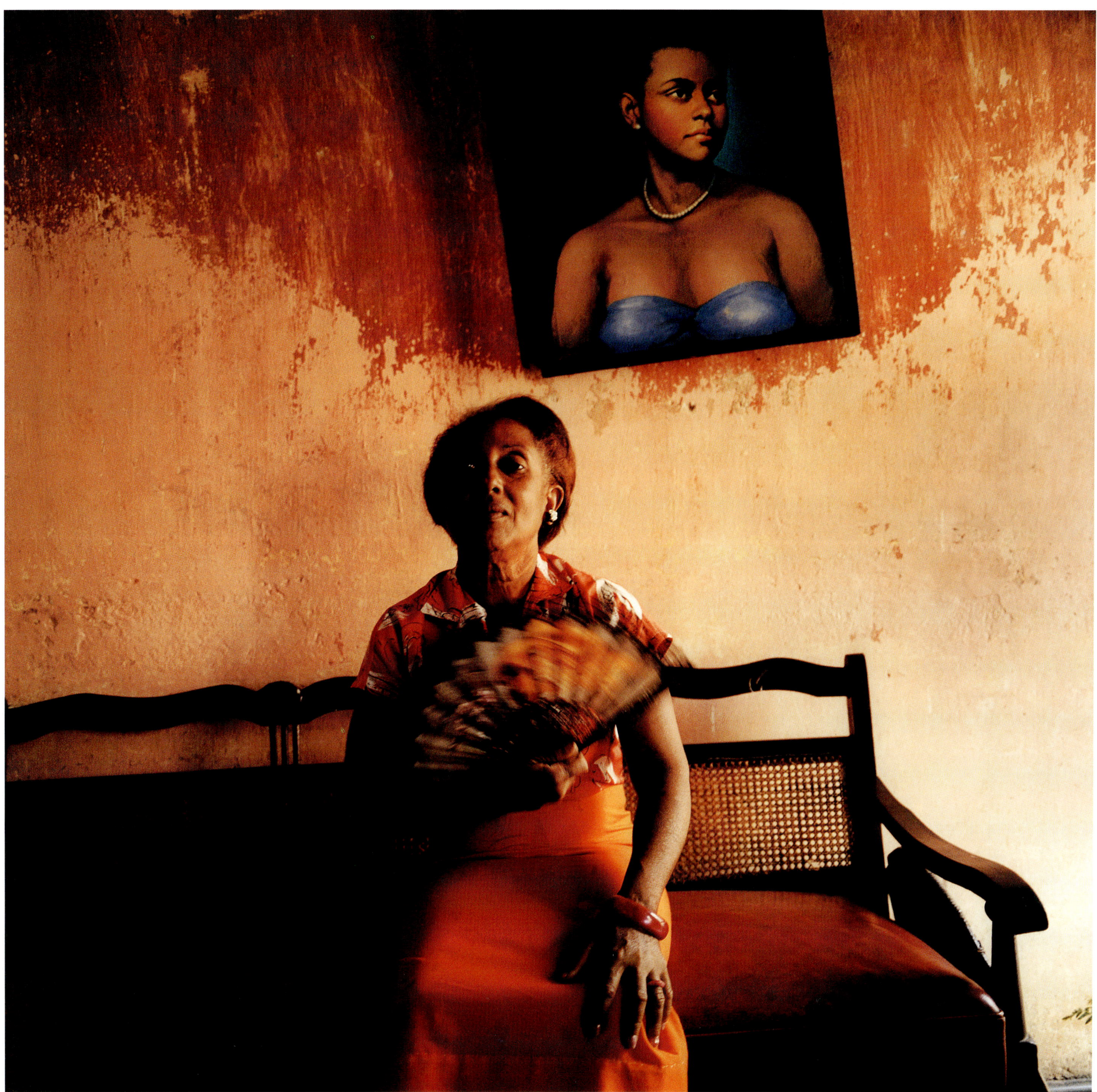

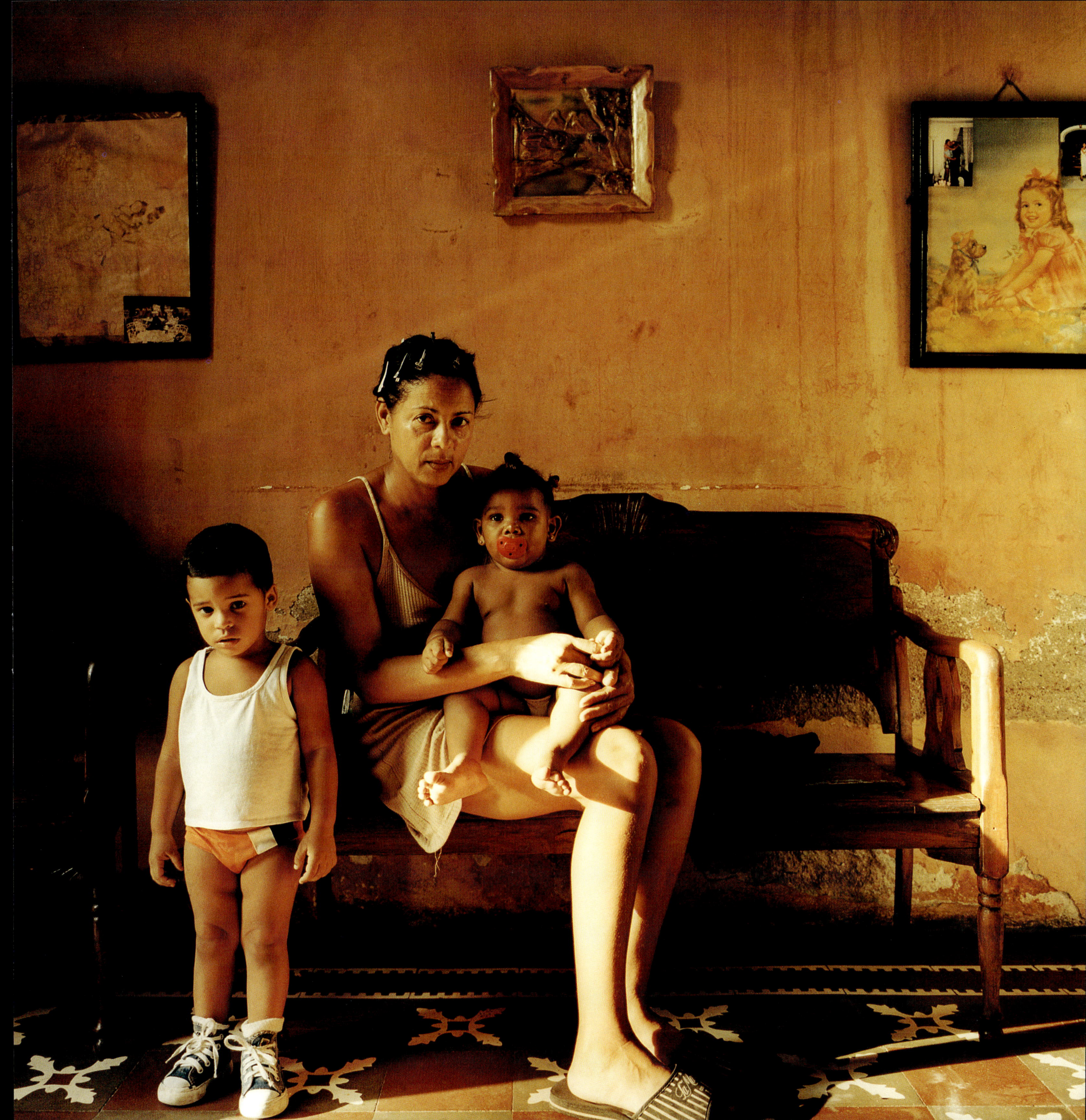

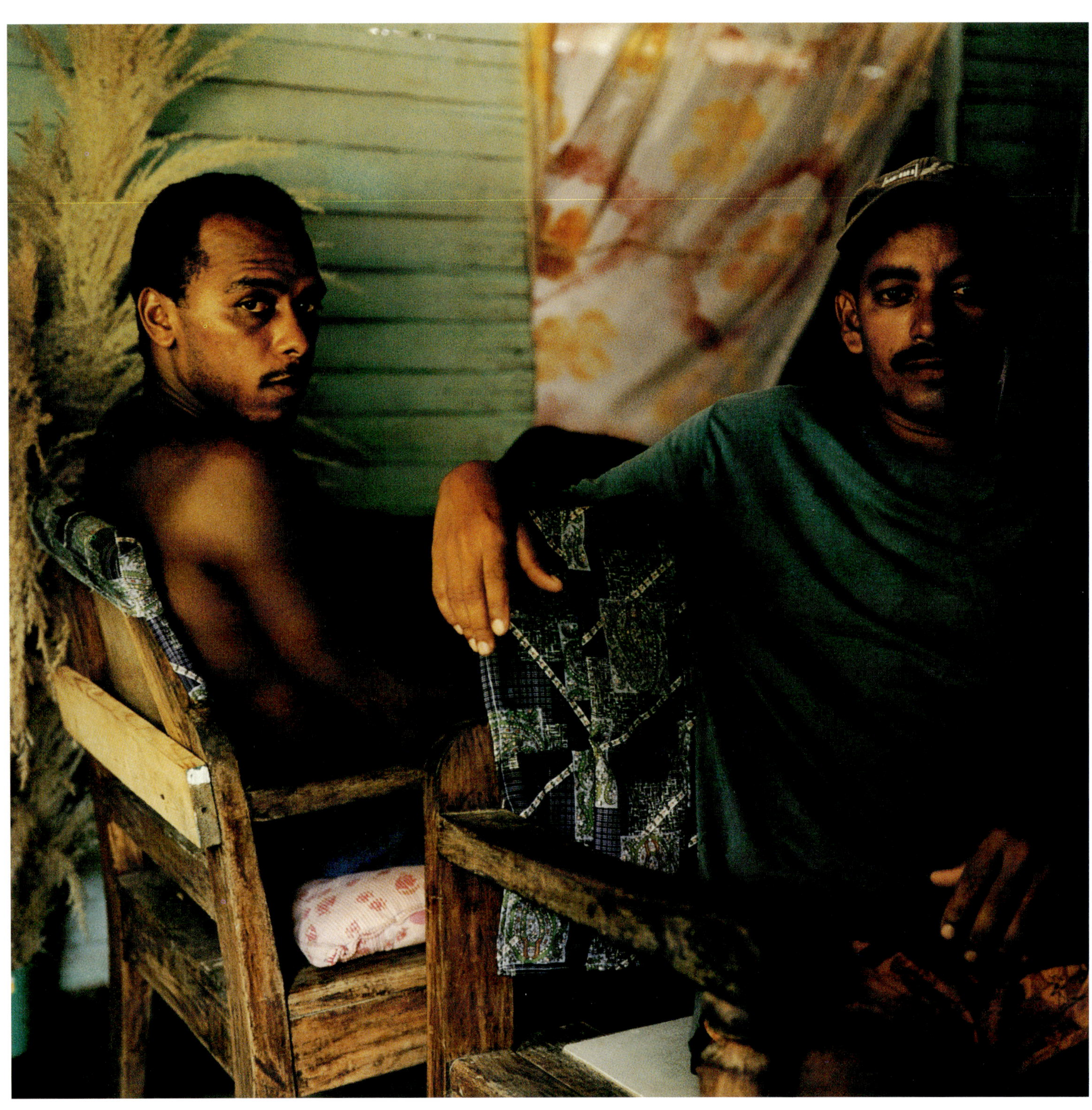

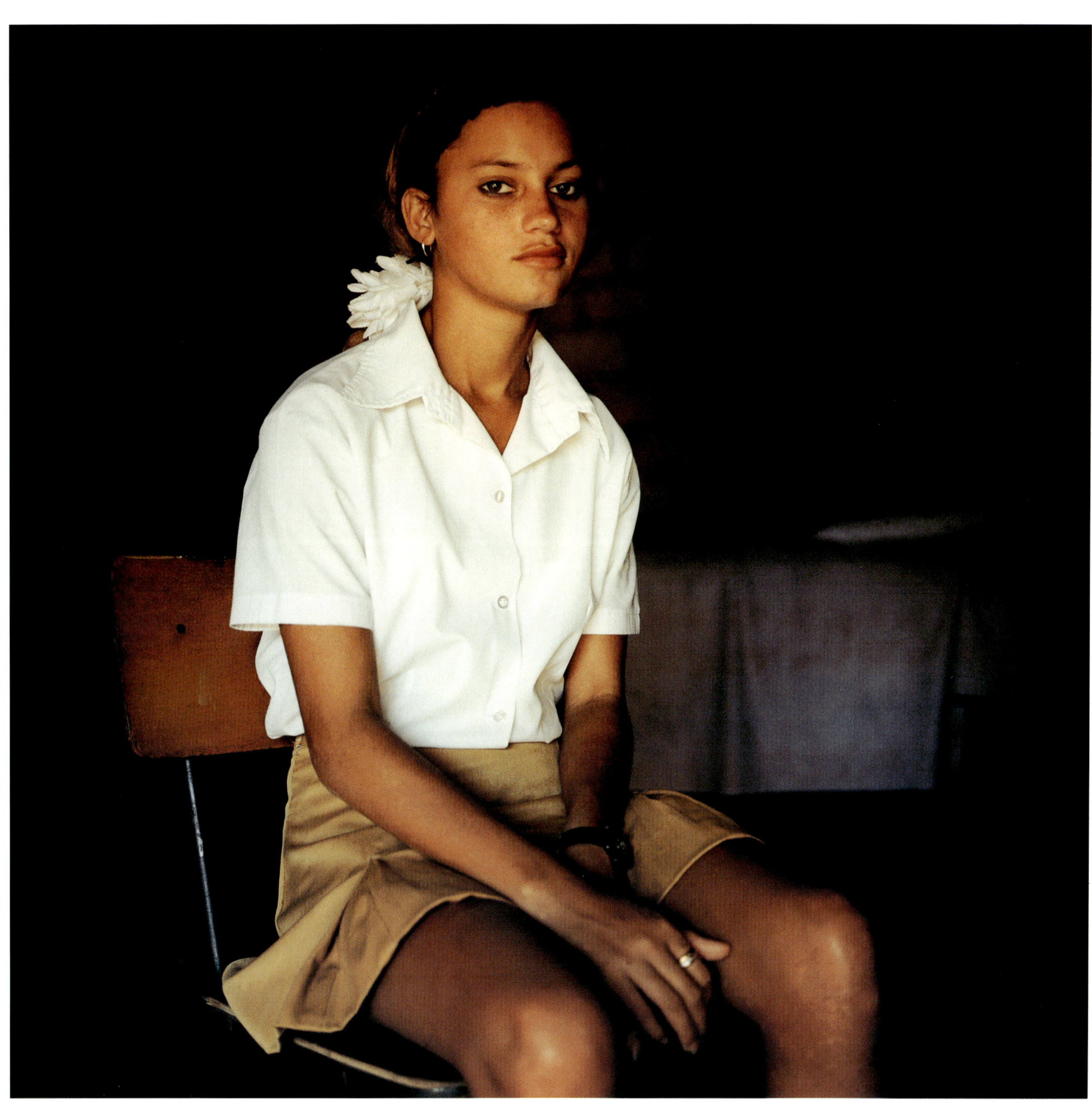

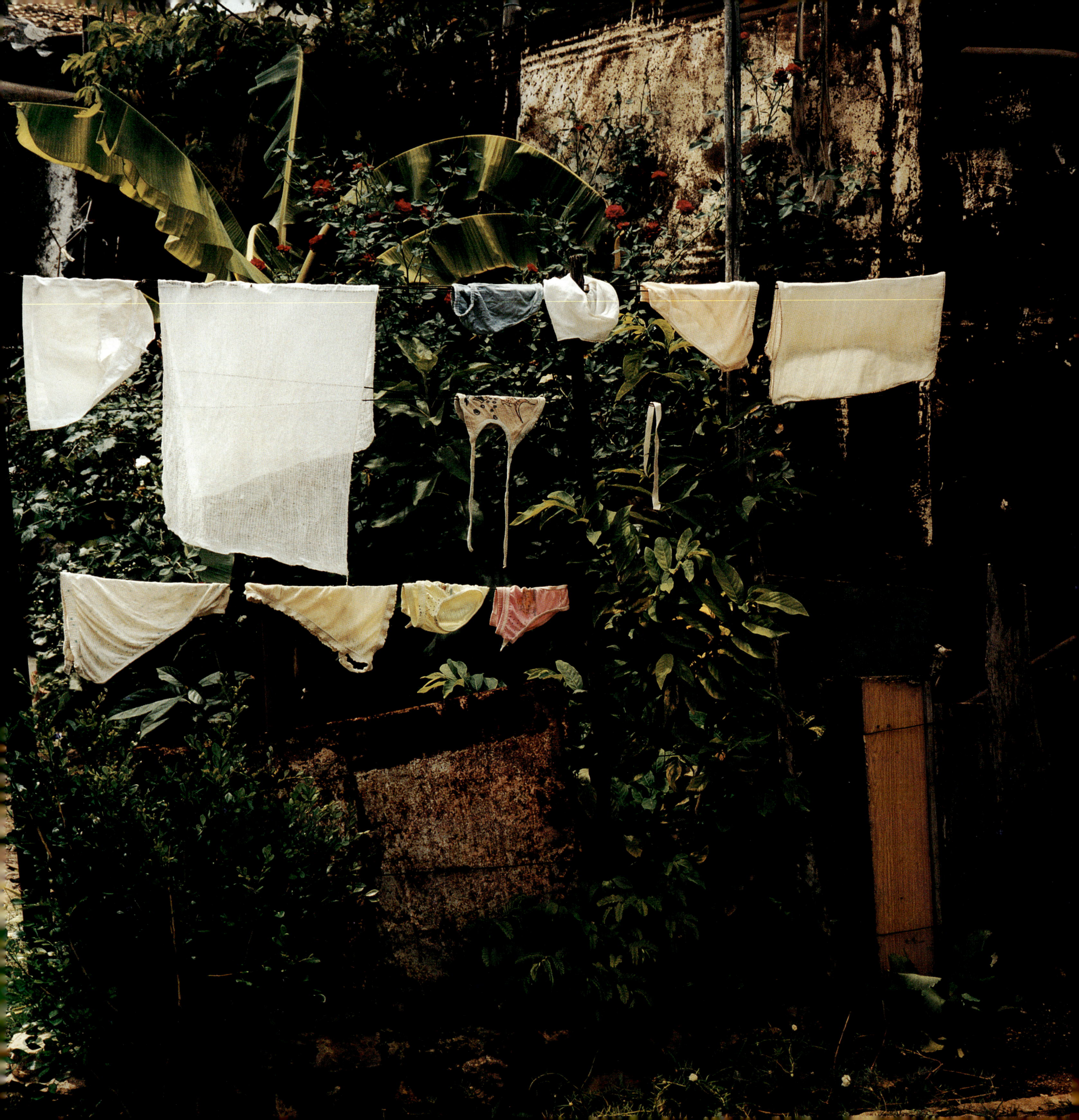

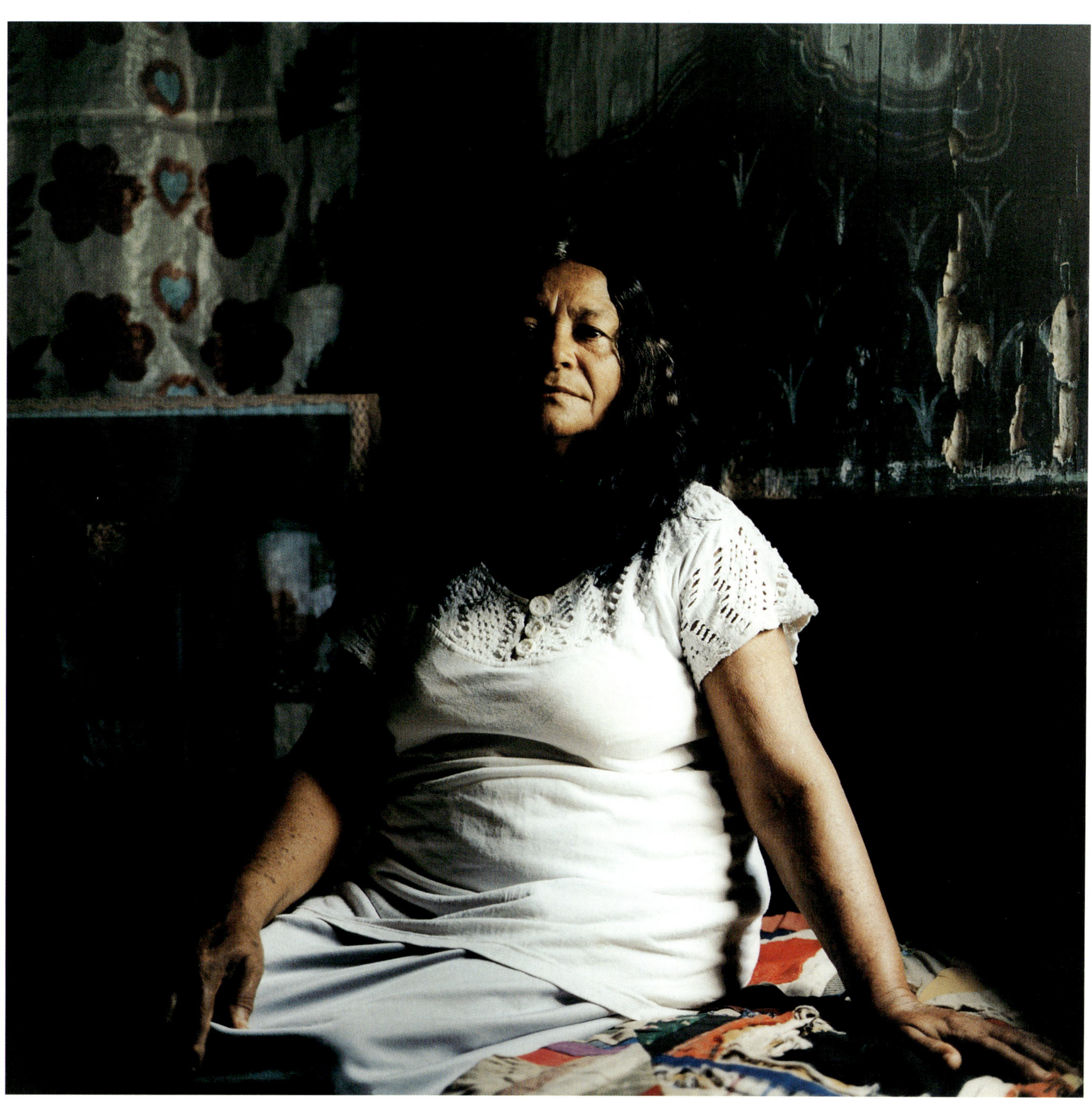

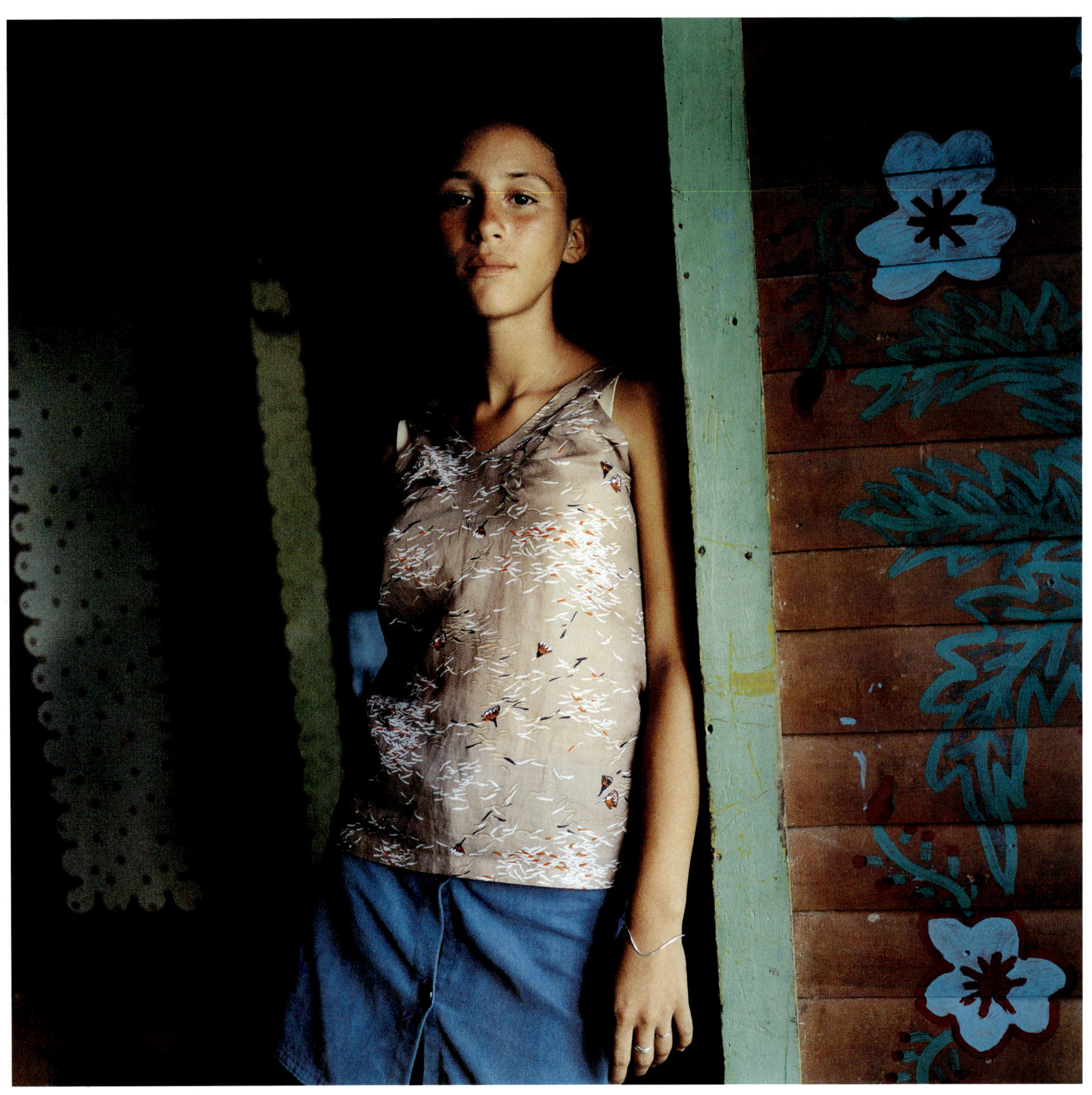

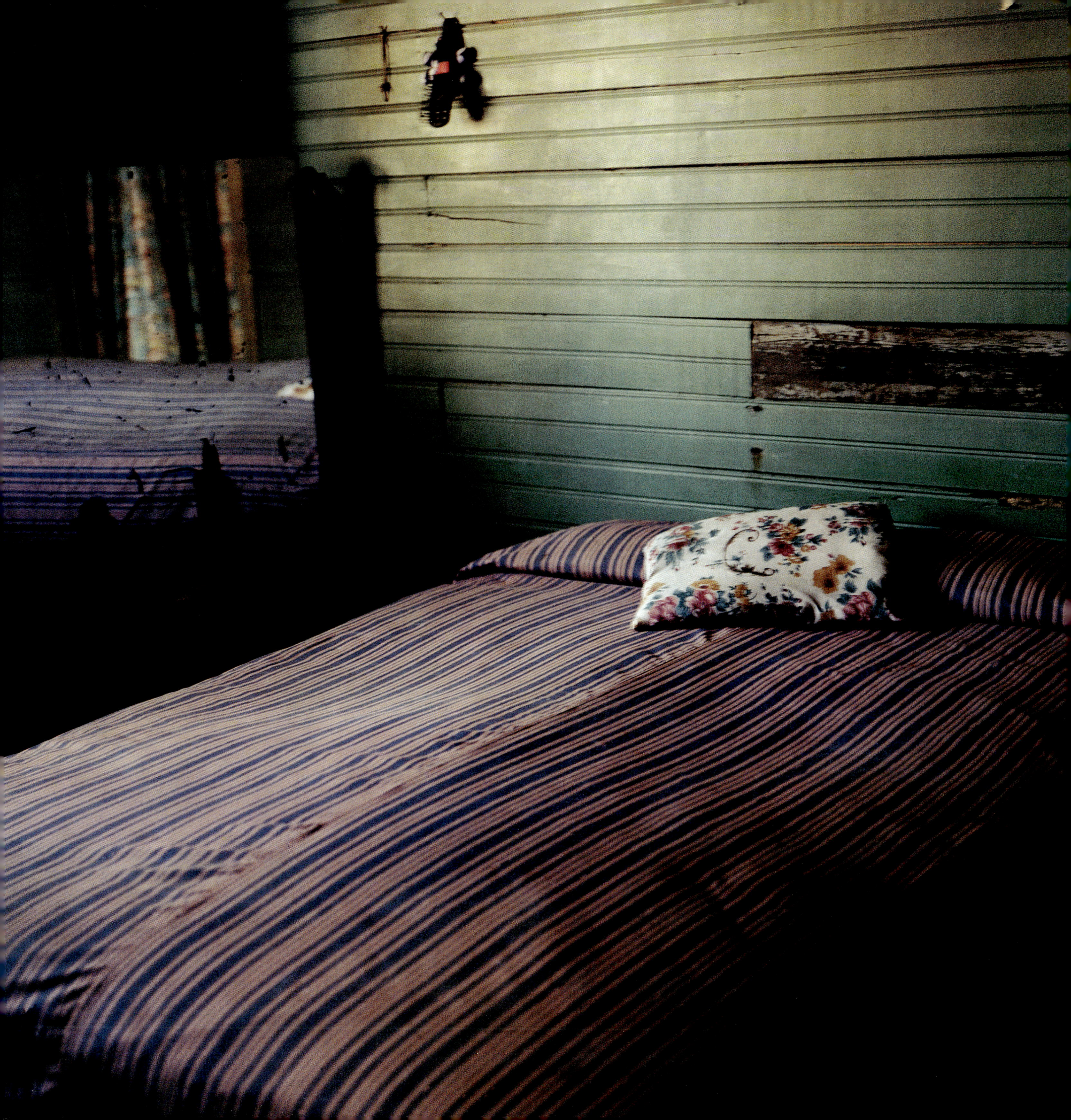

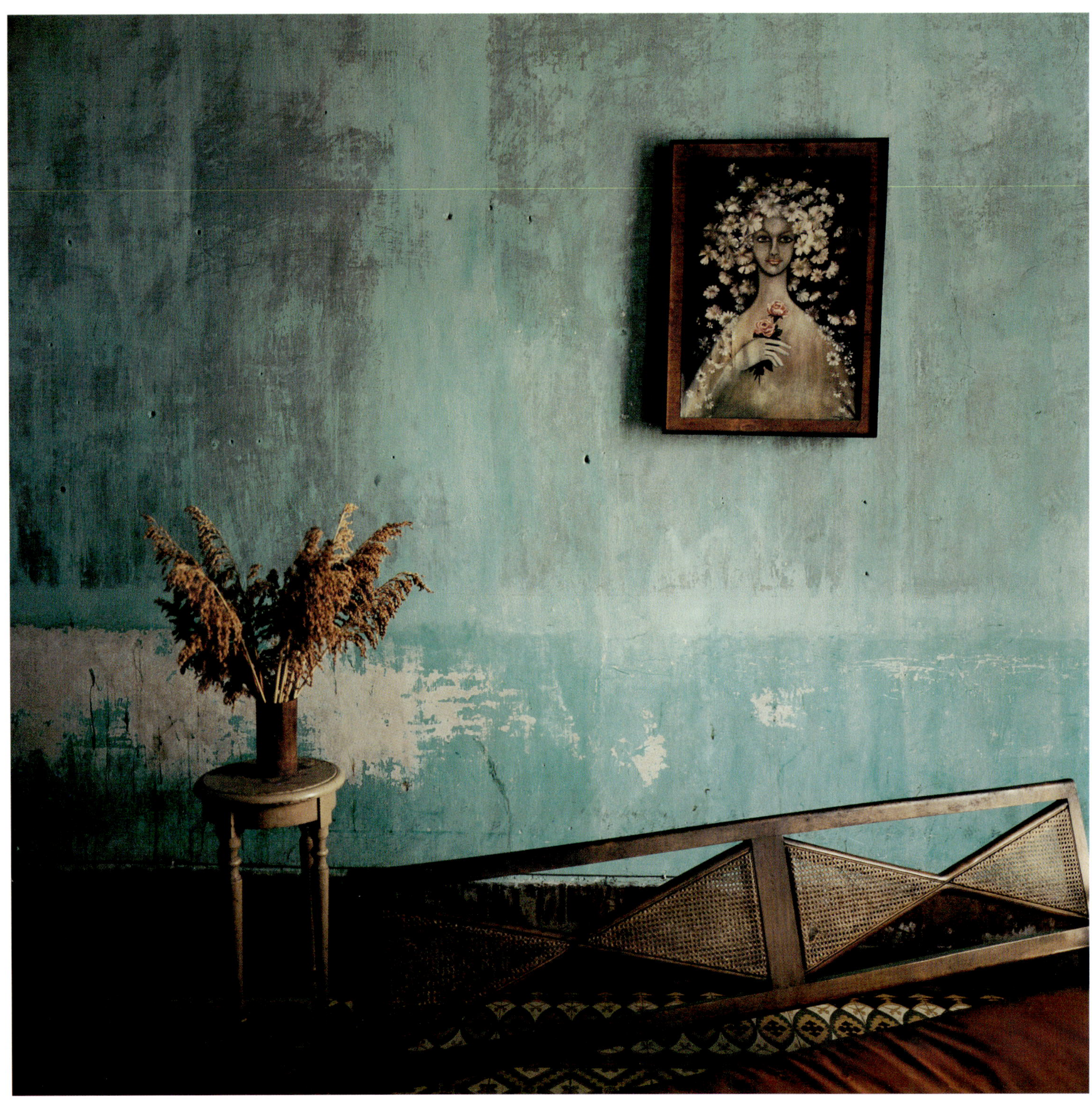

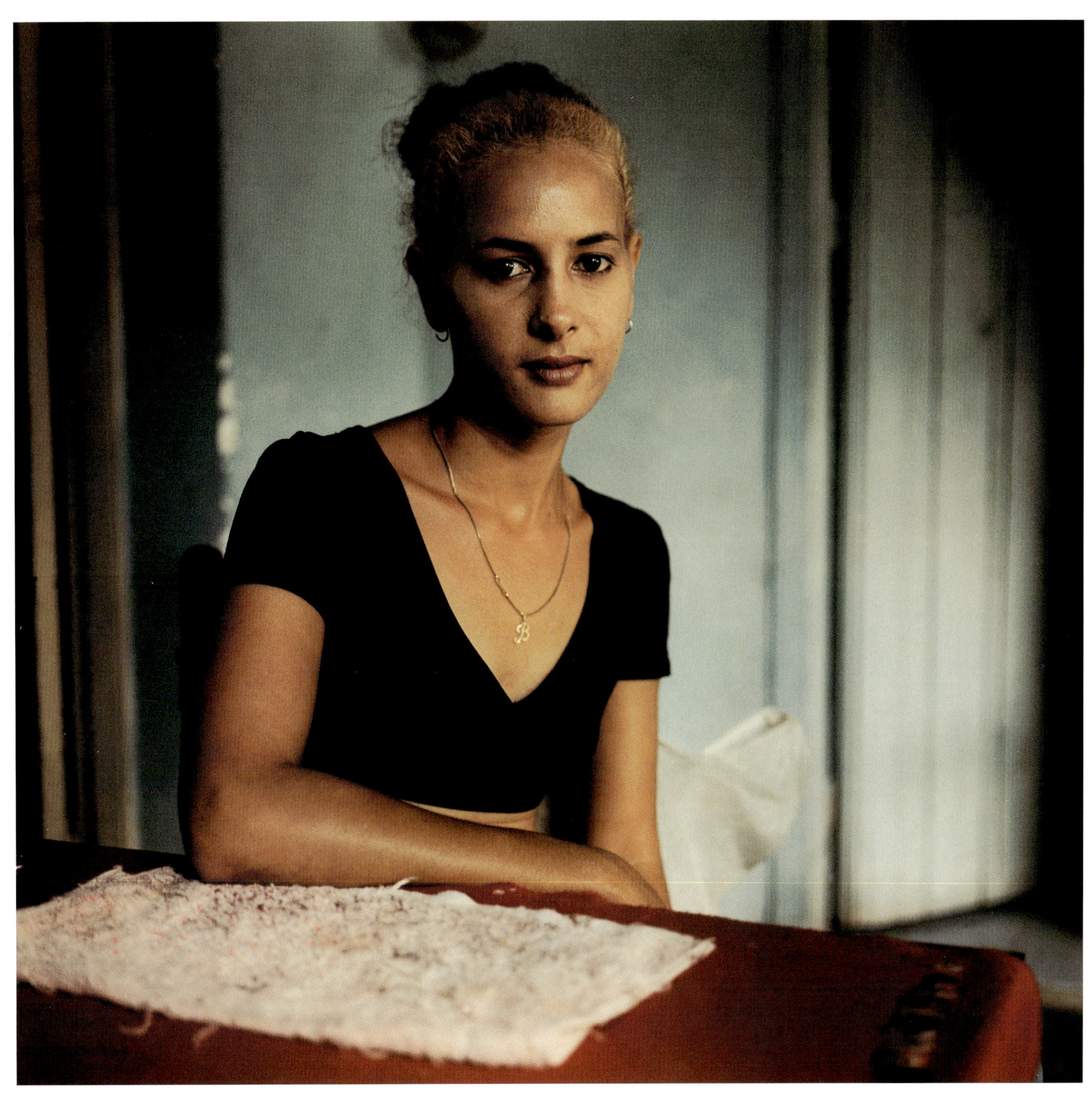

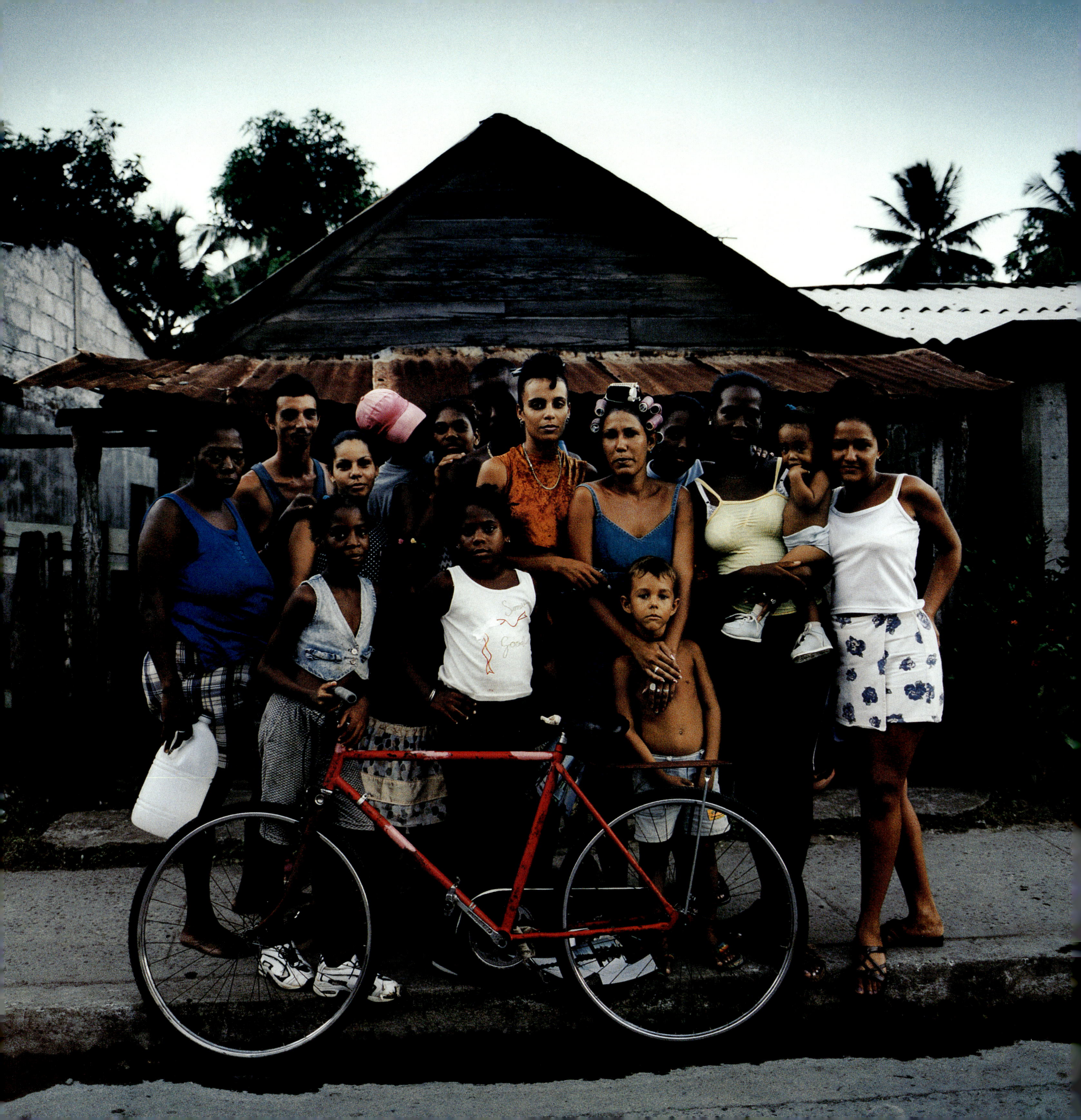

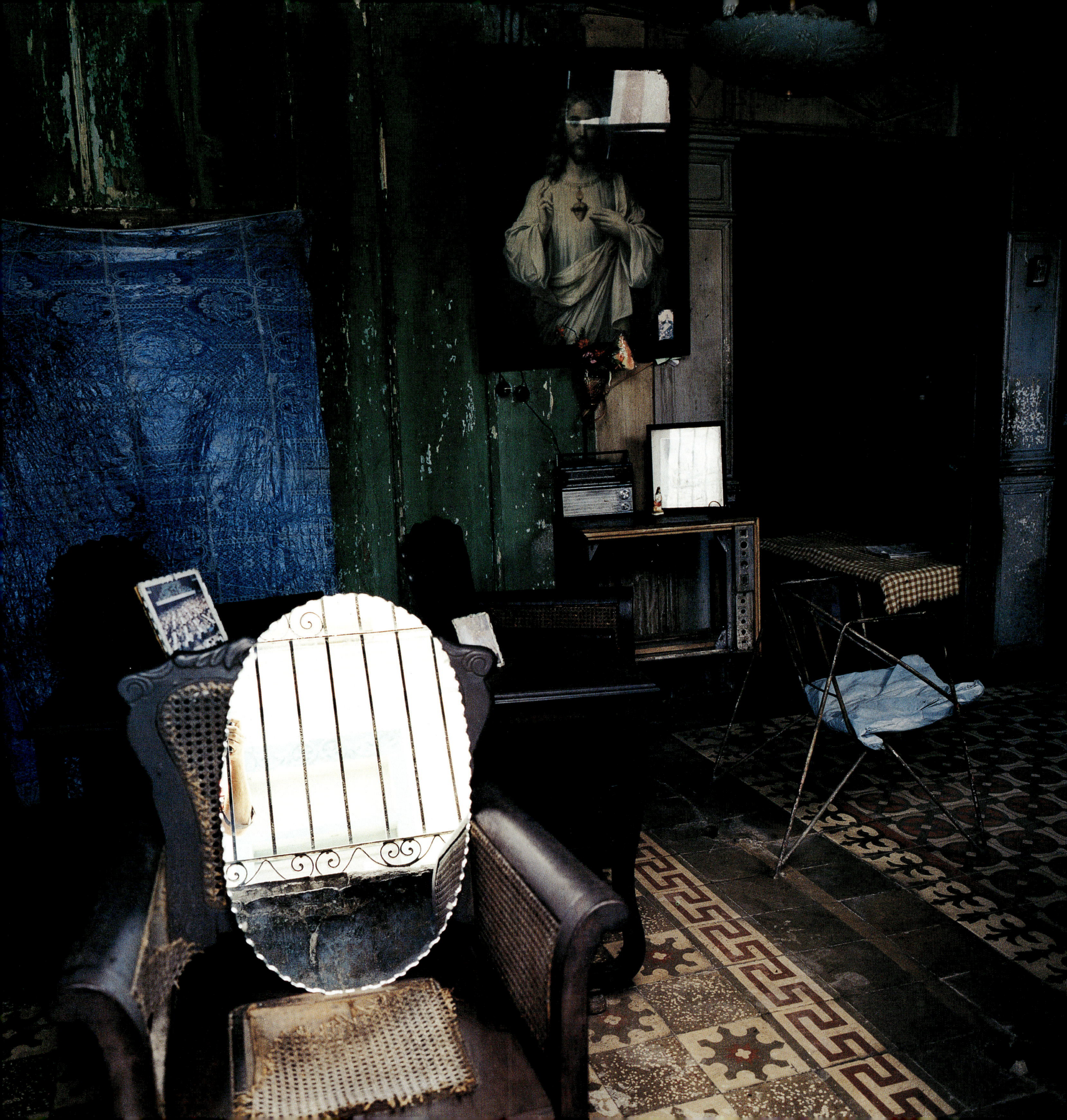

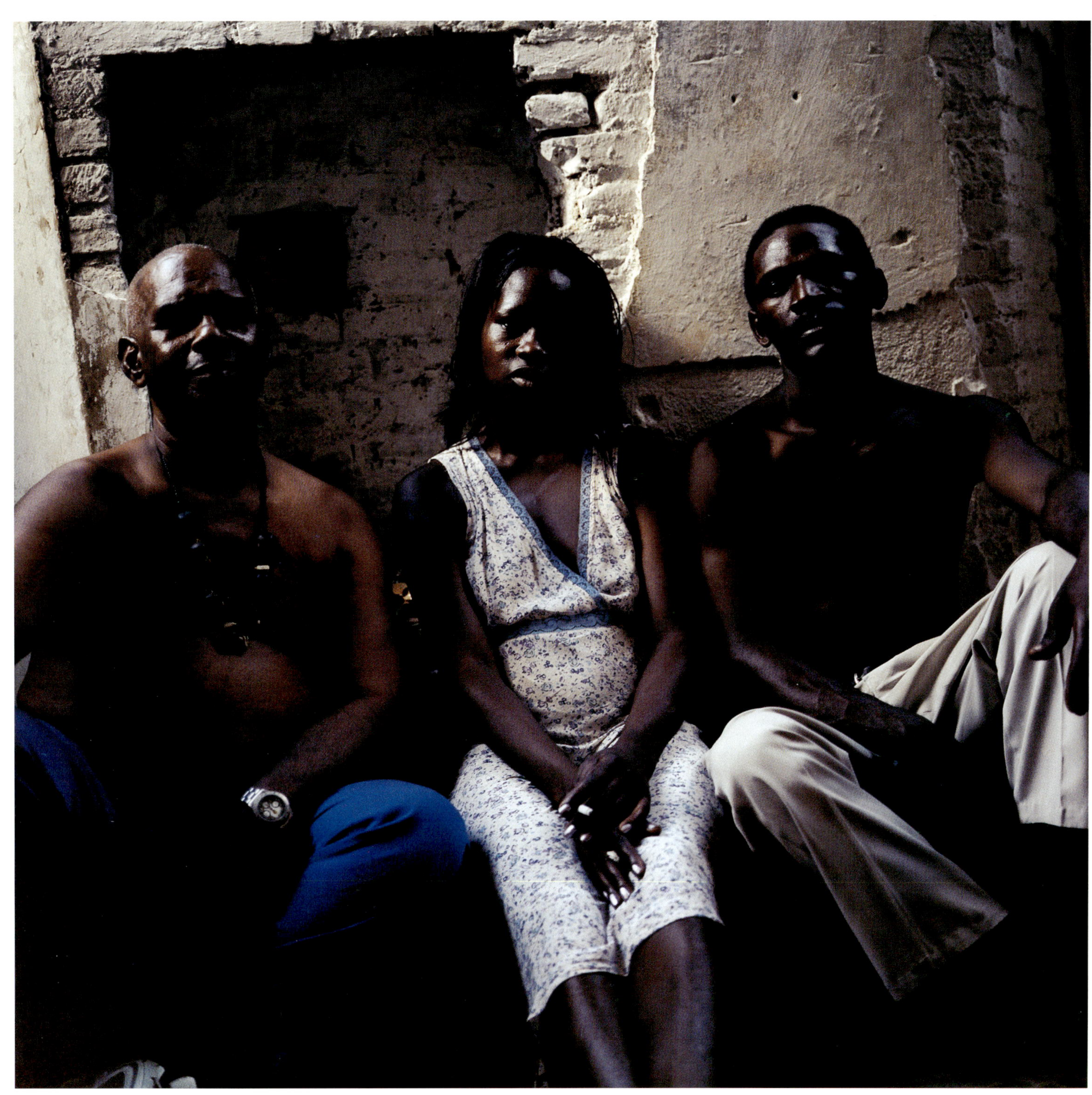

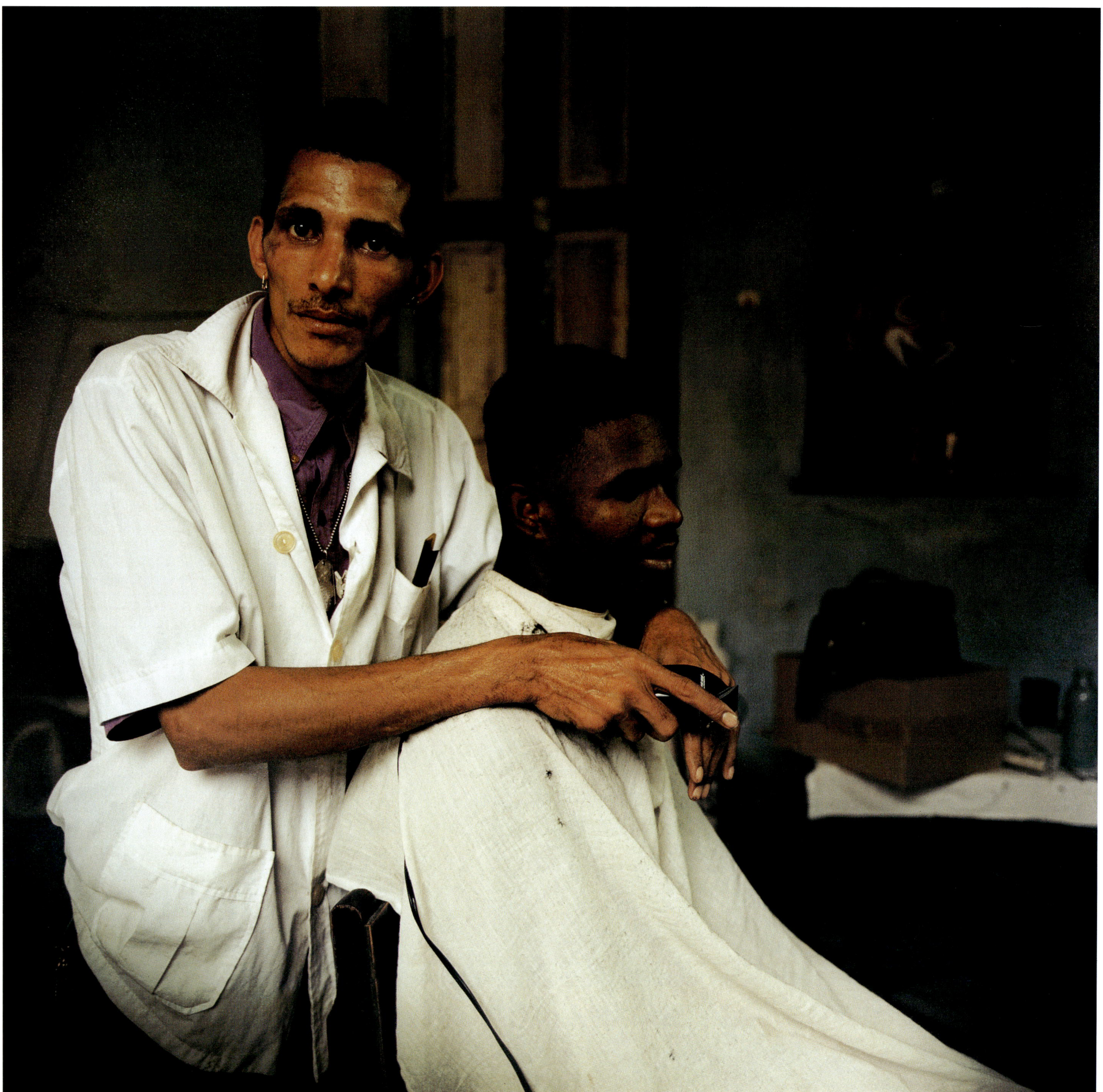

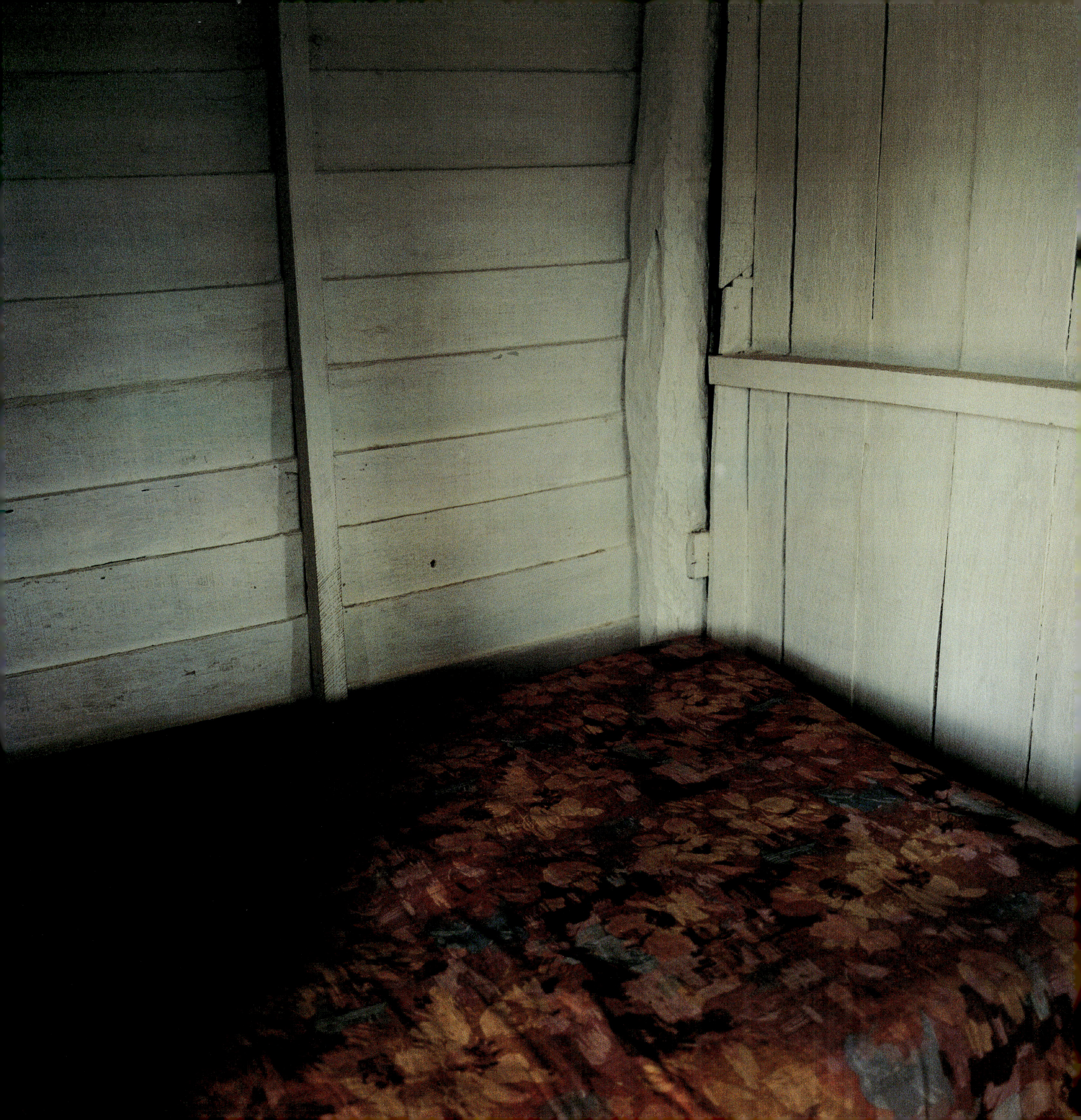

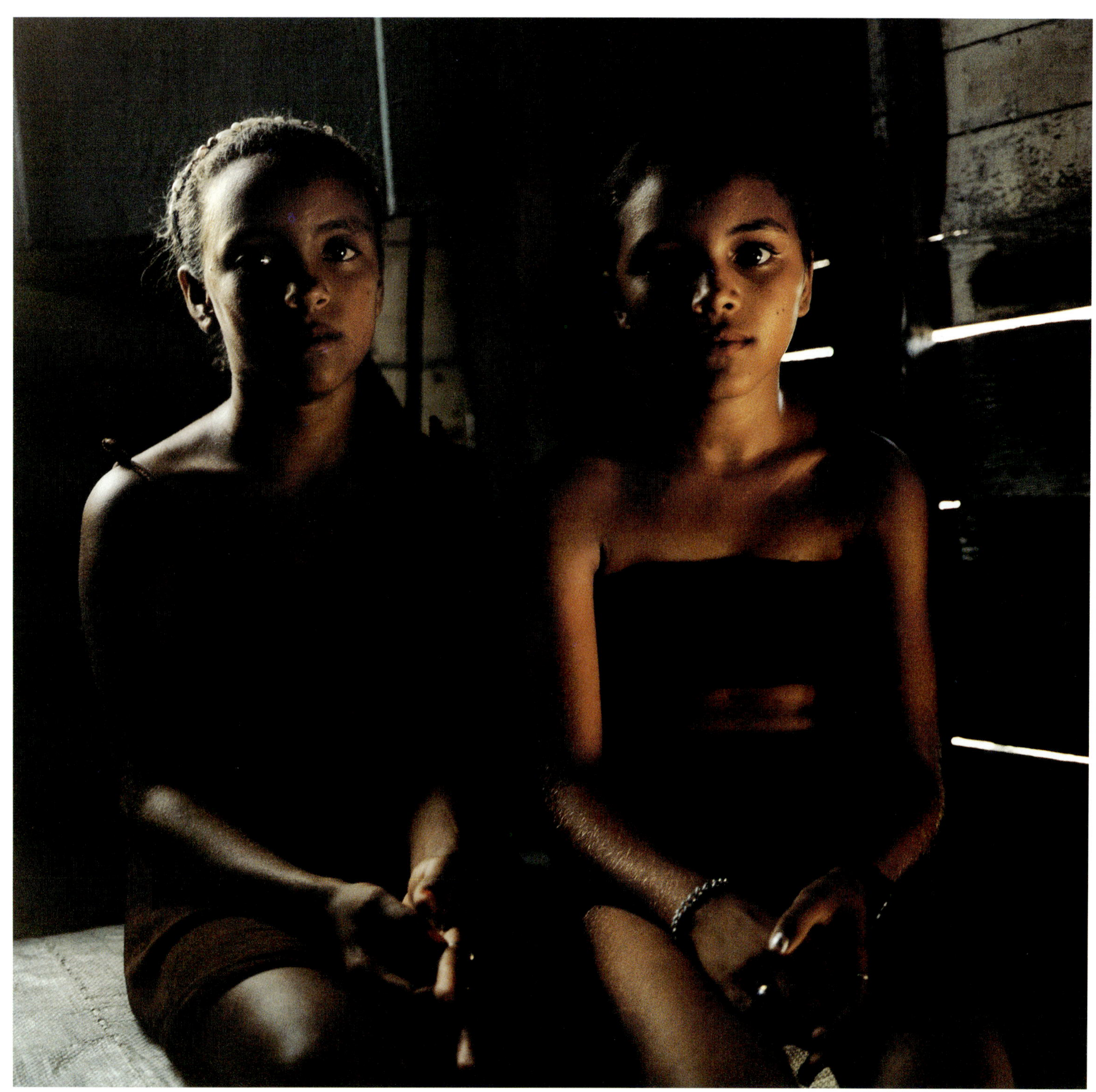

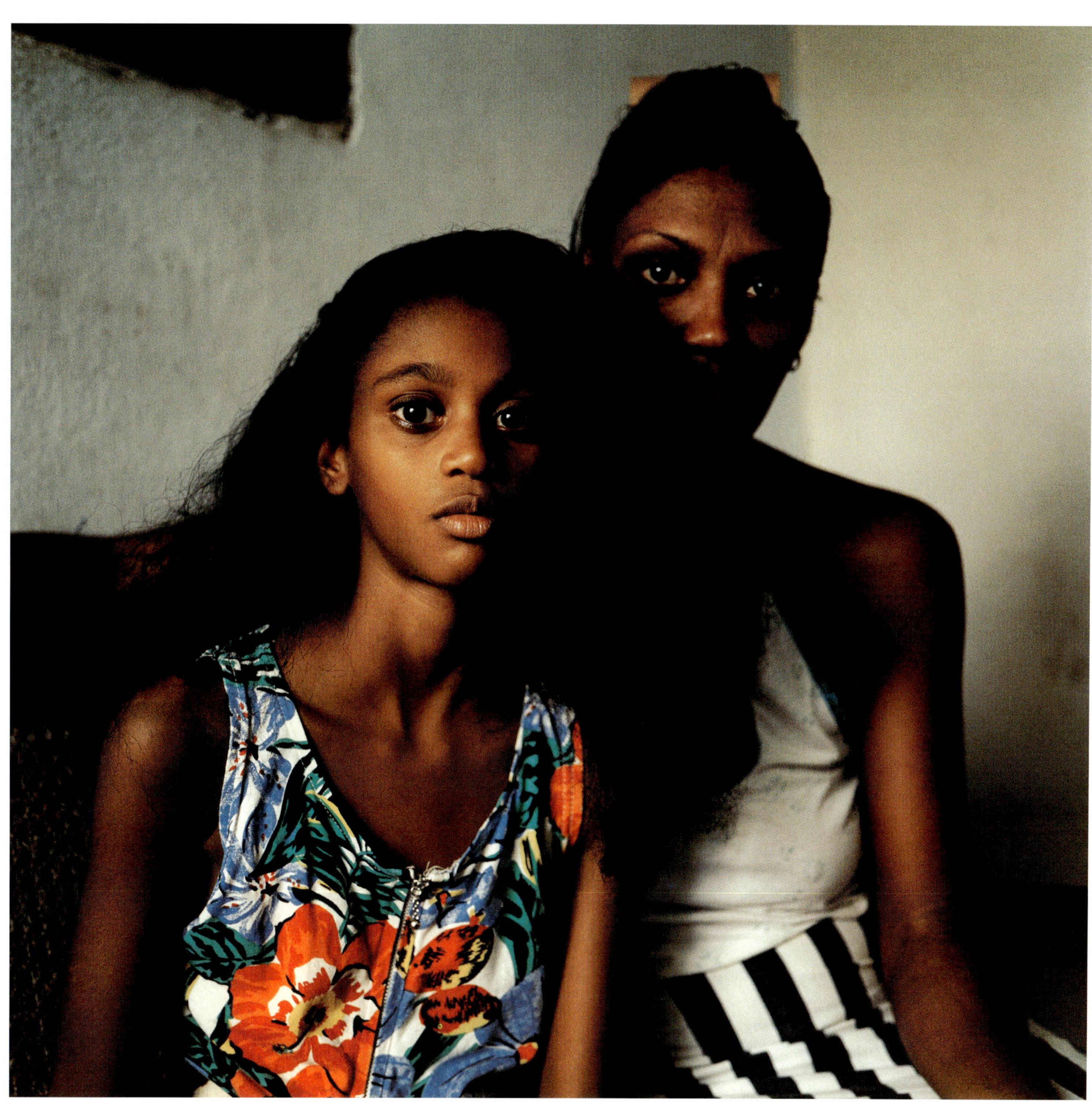

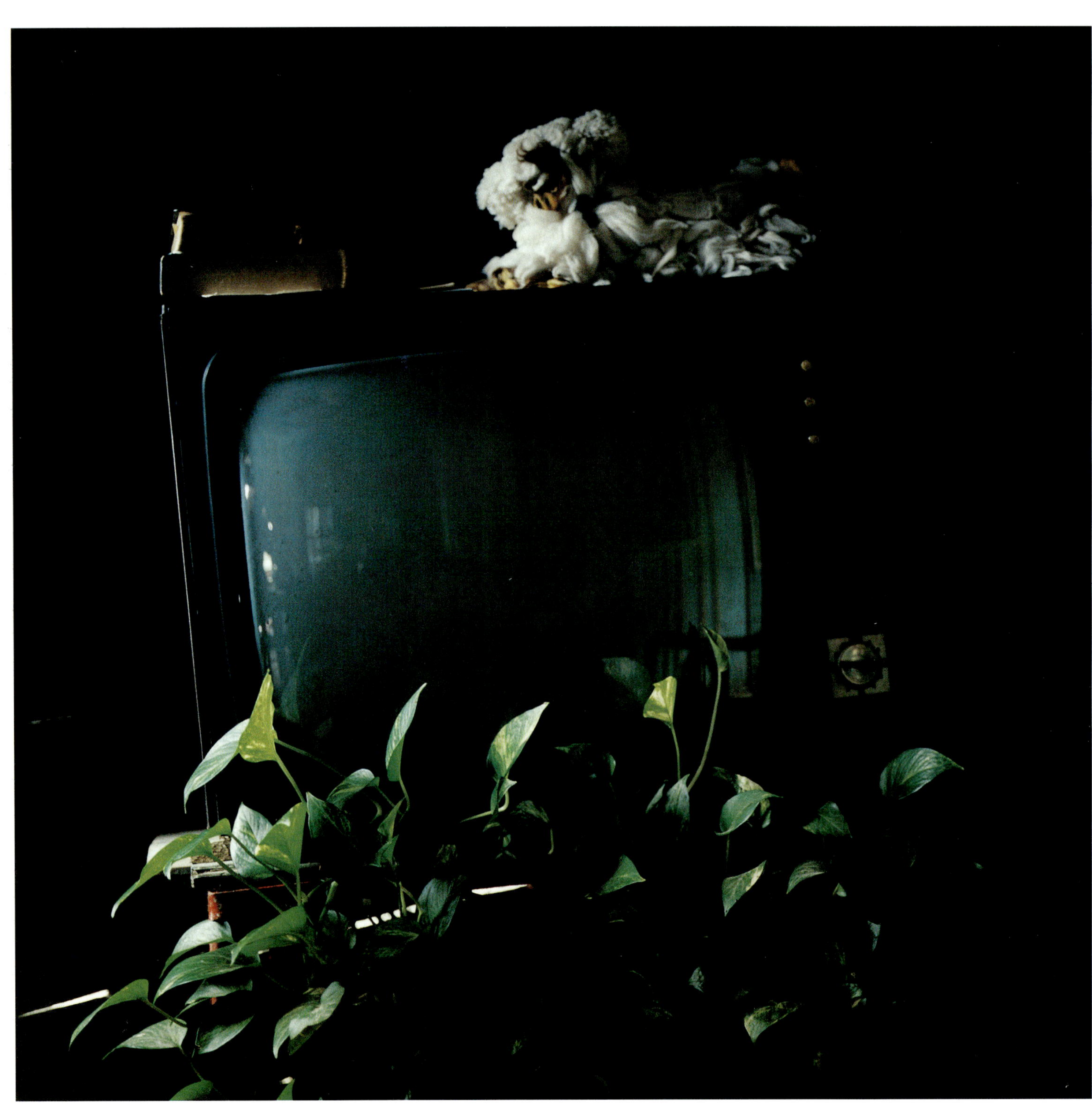

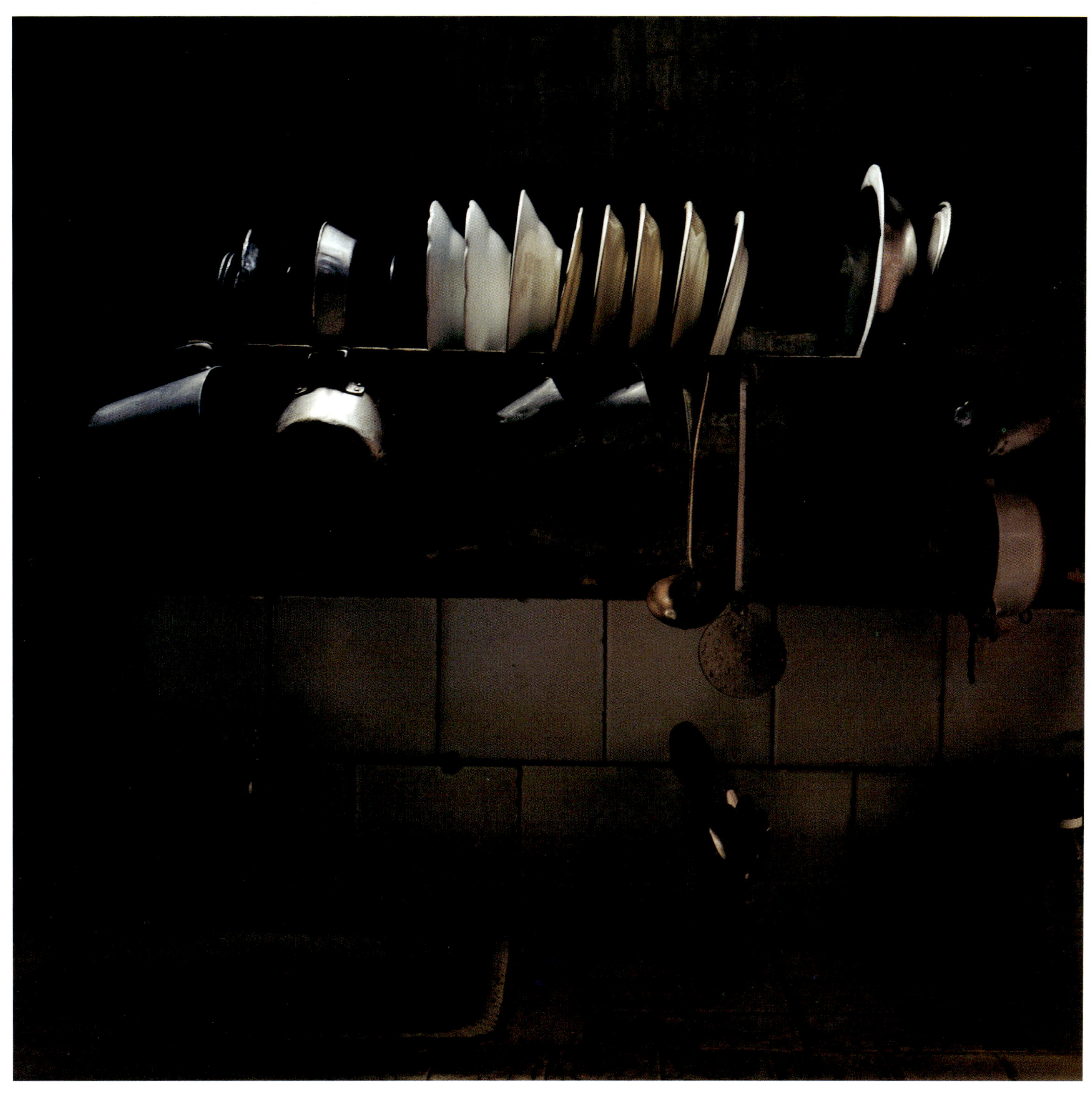

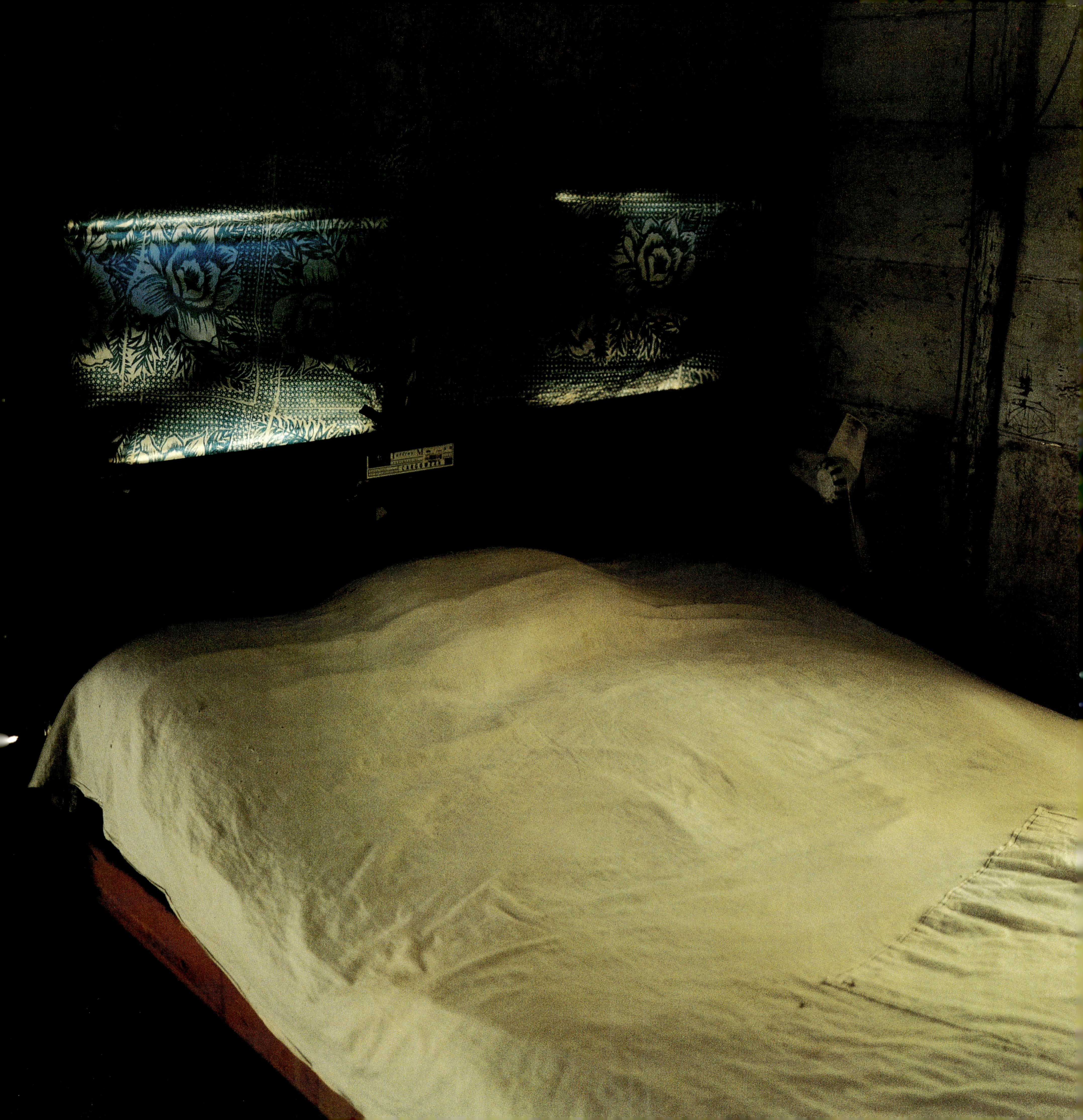

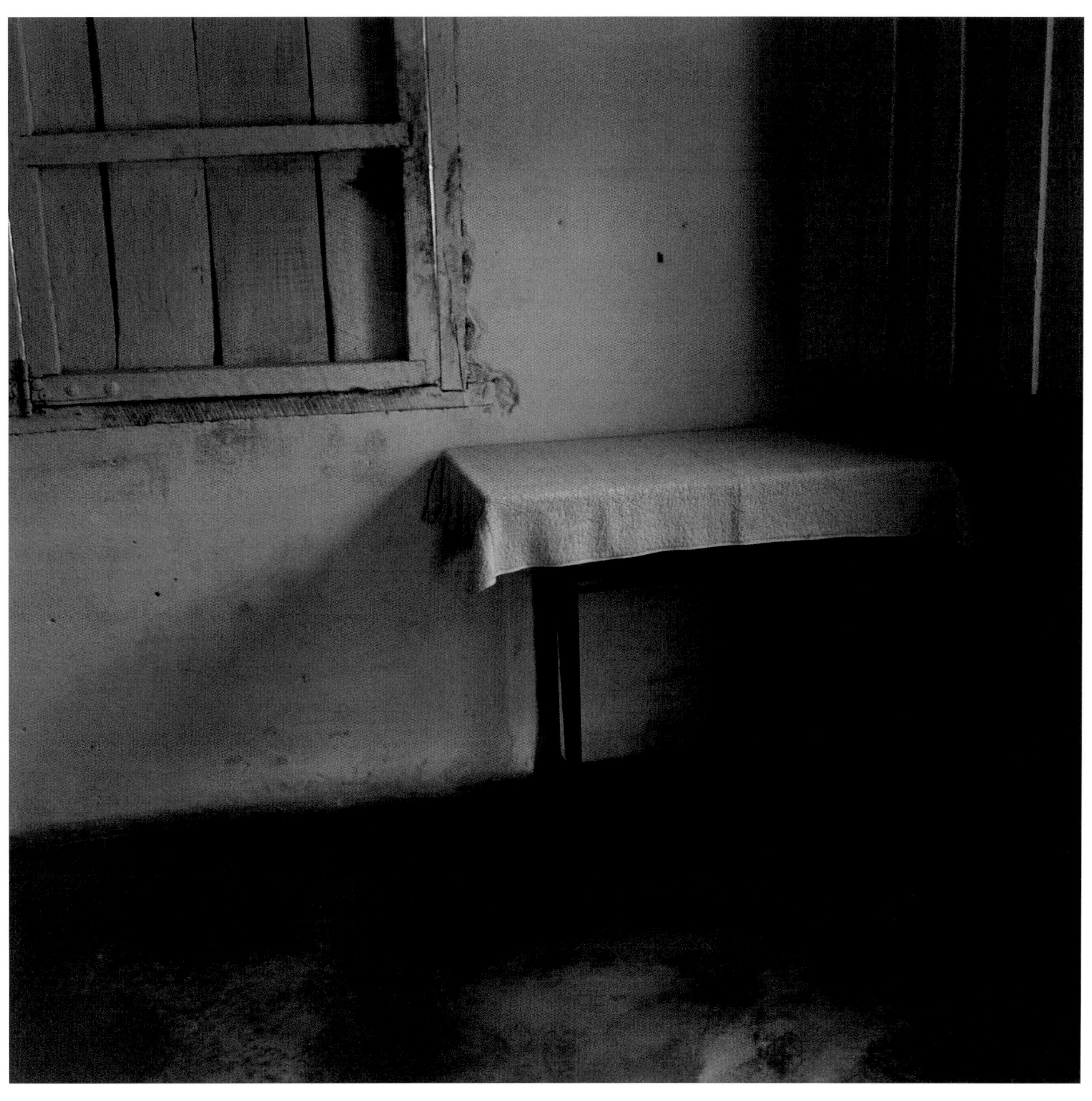

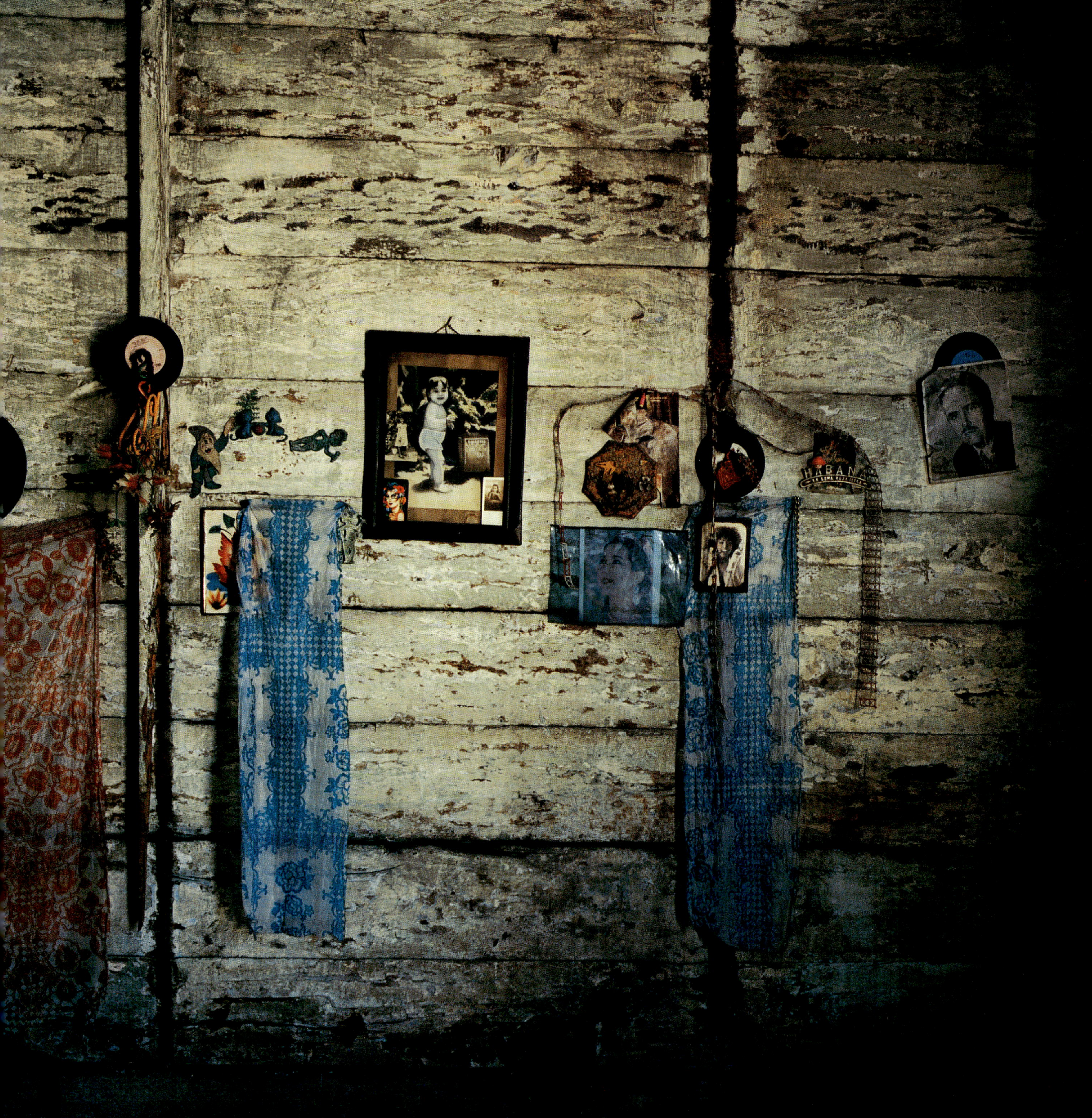

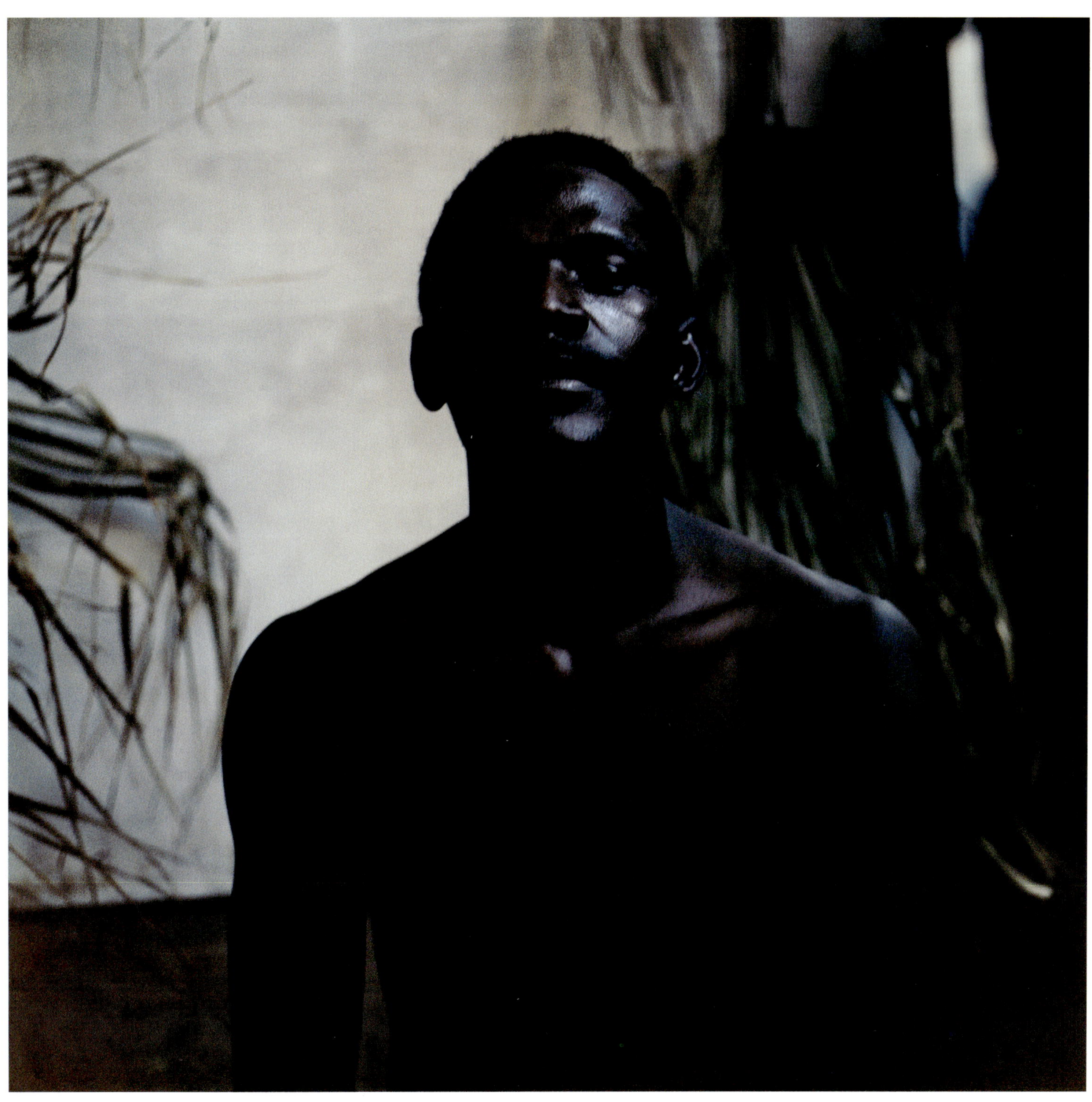

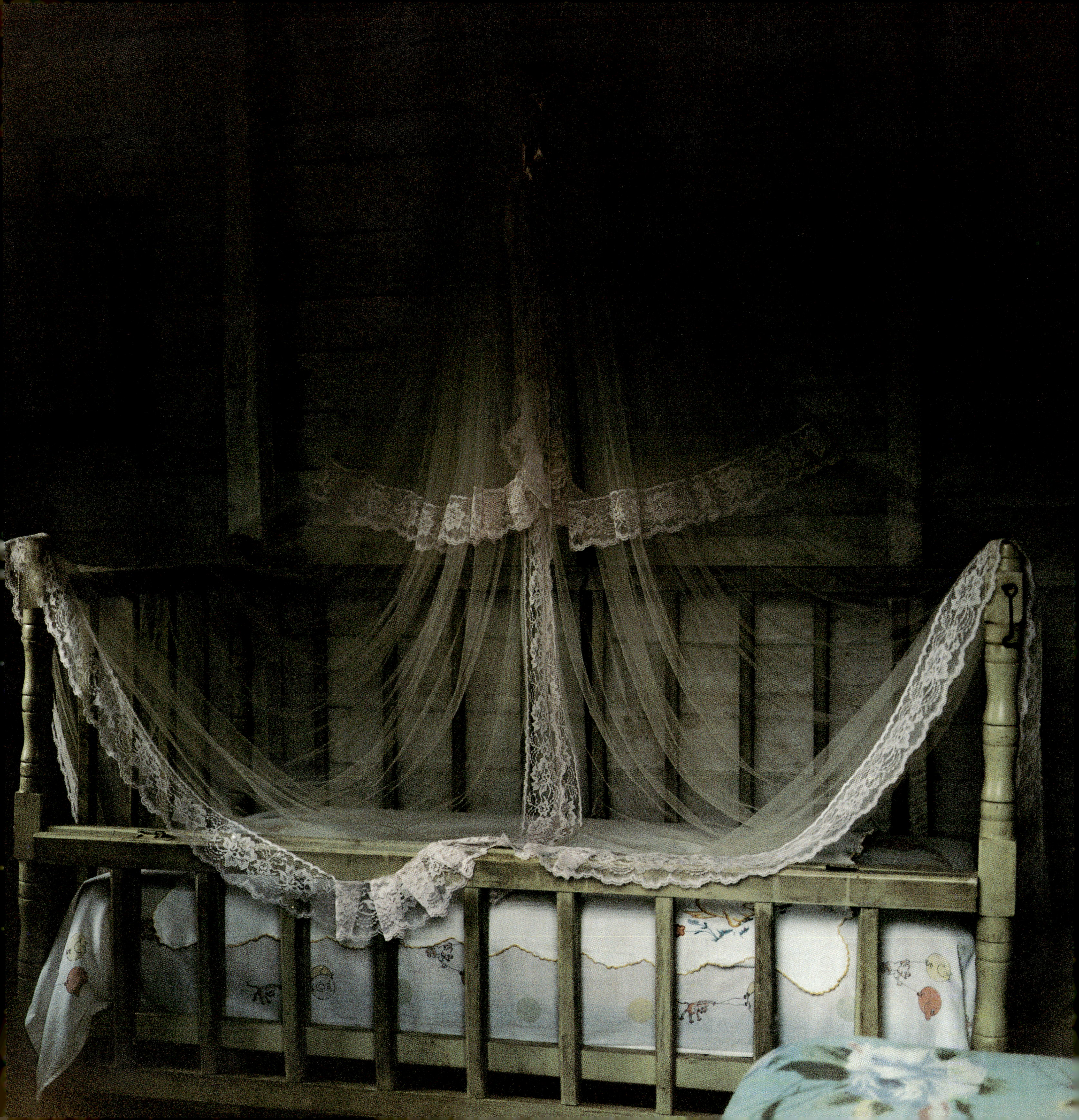

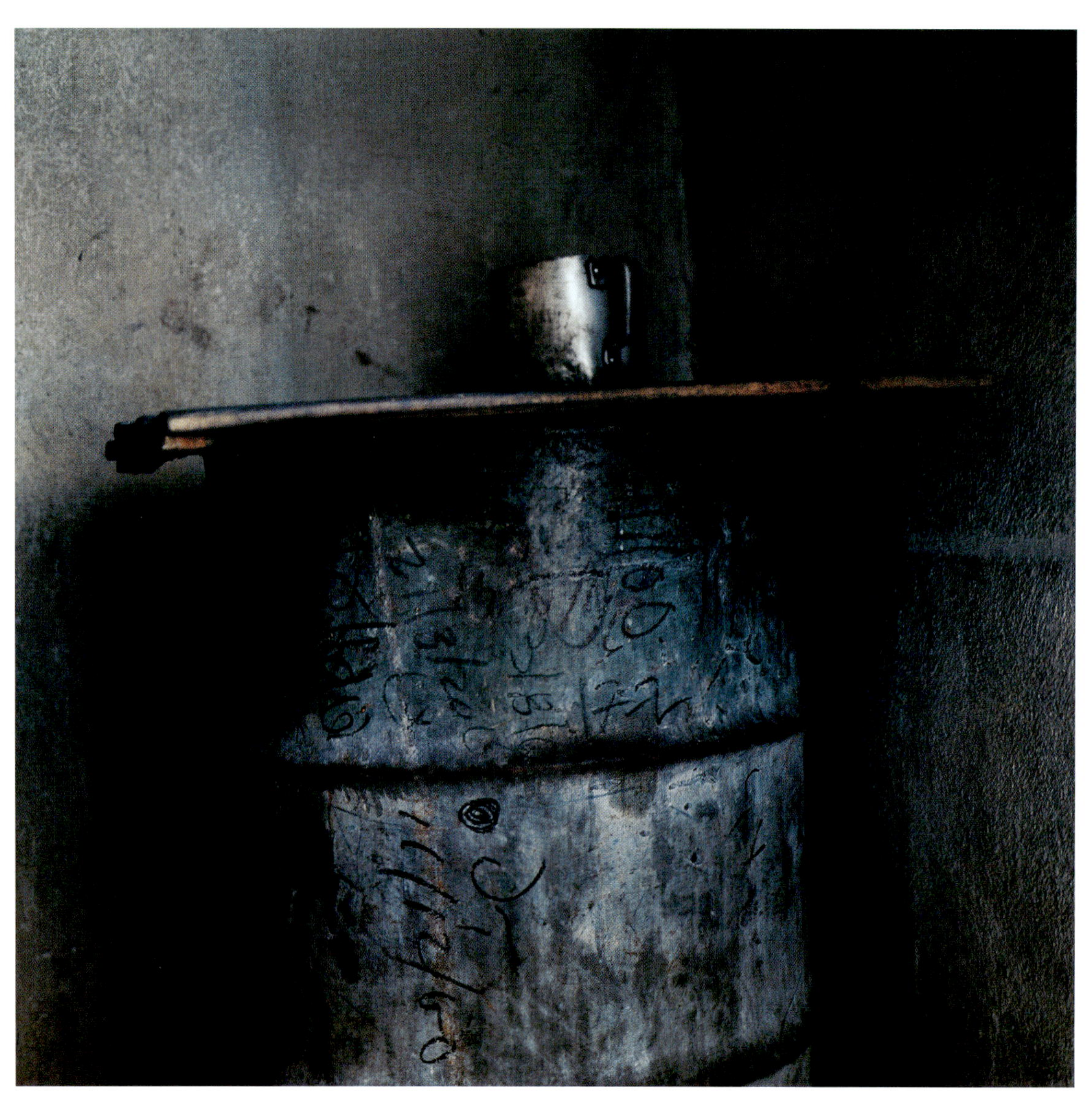

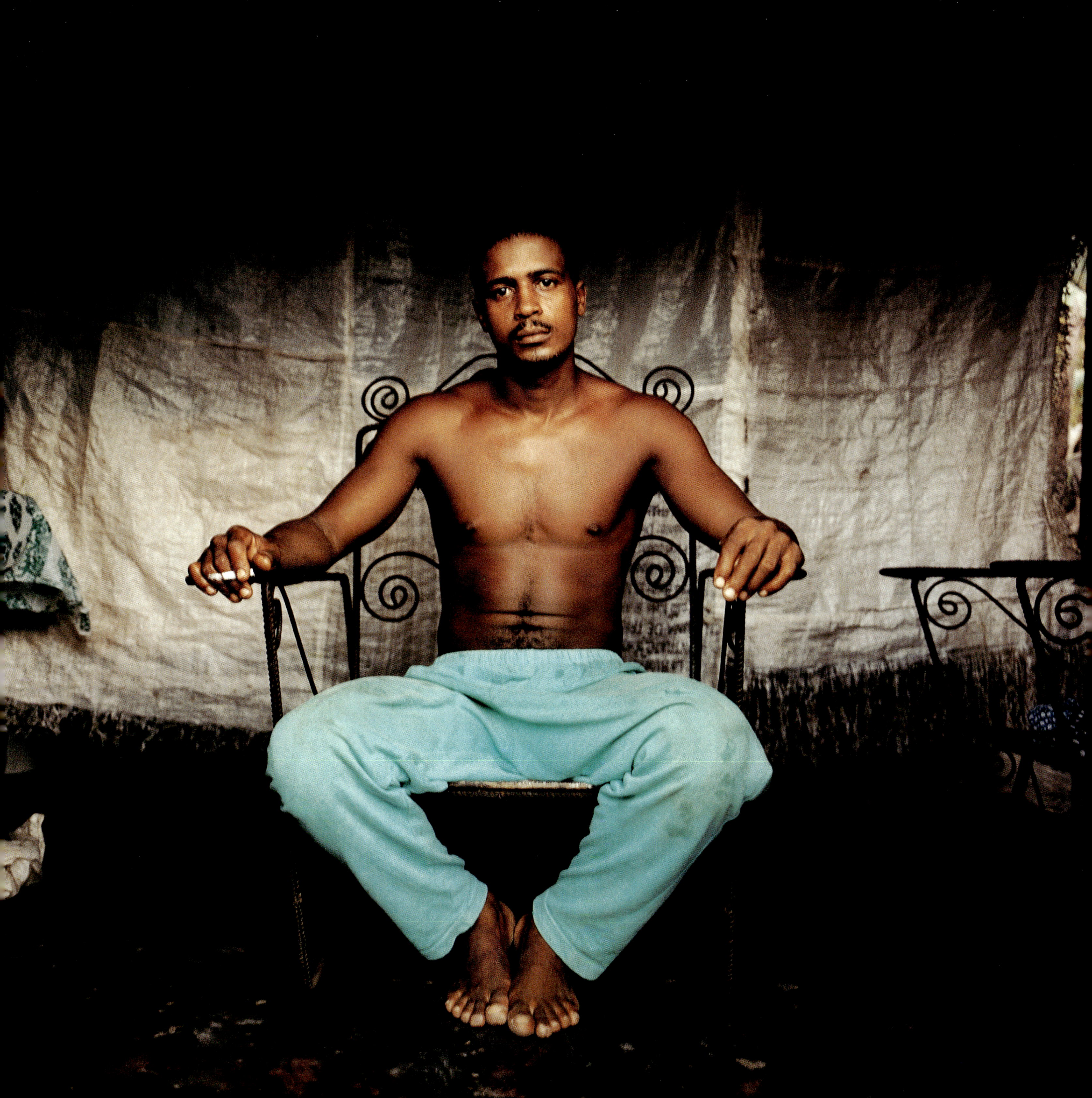

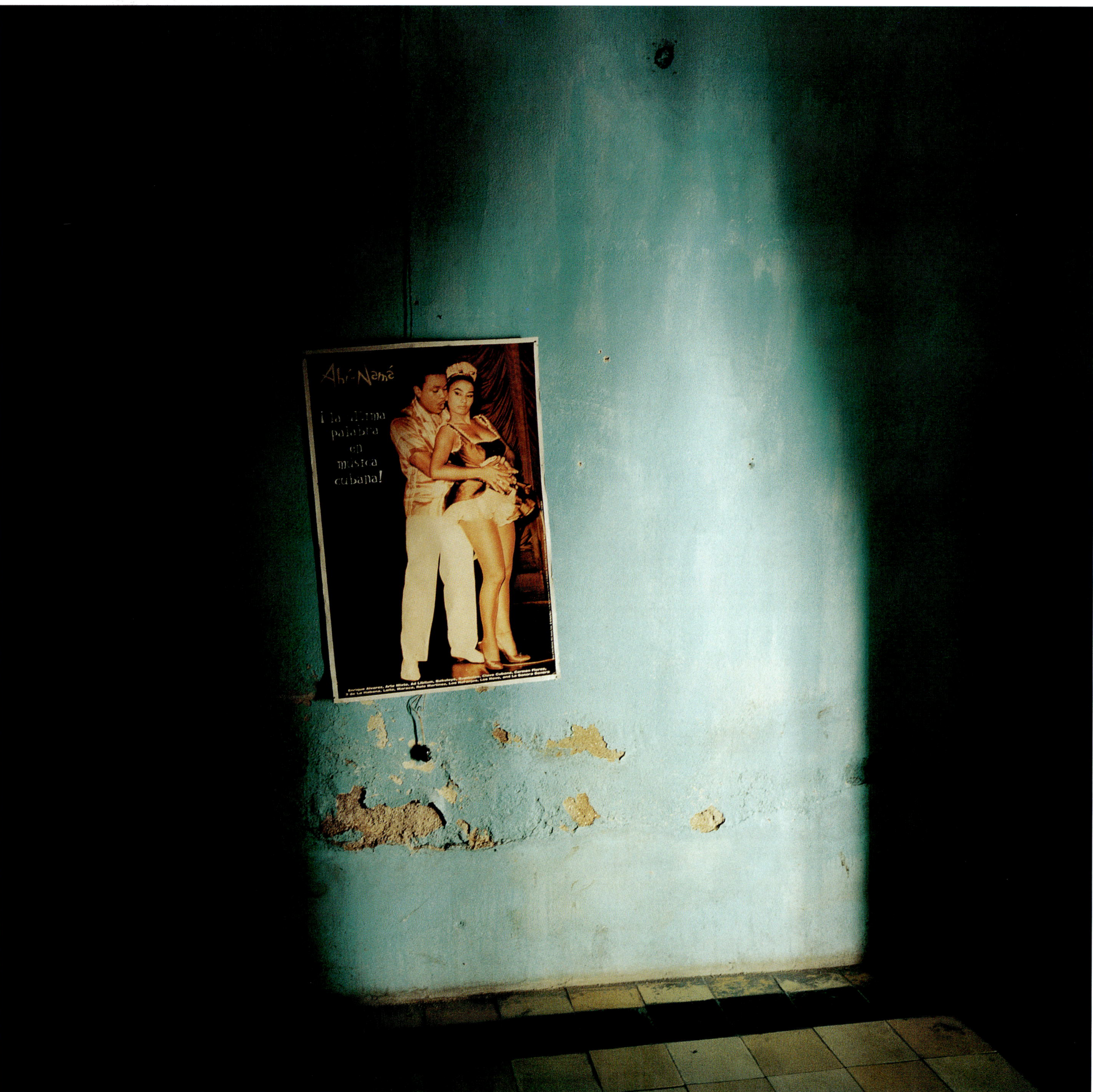
Ahí-Namá
¡la última
palabra
en
música
cubana!

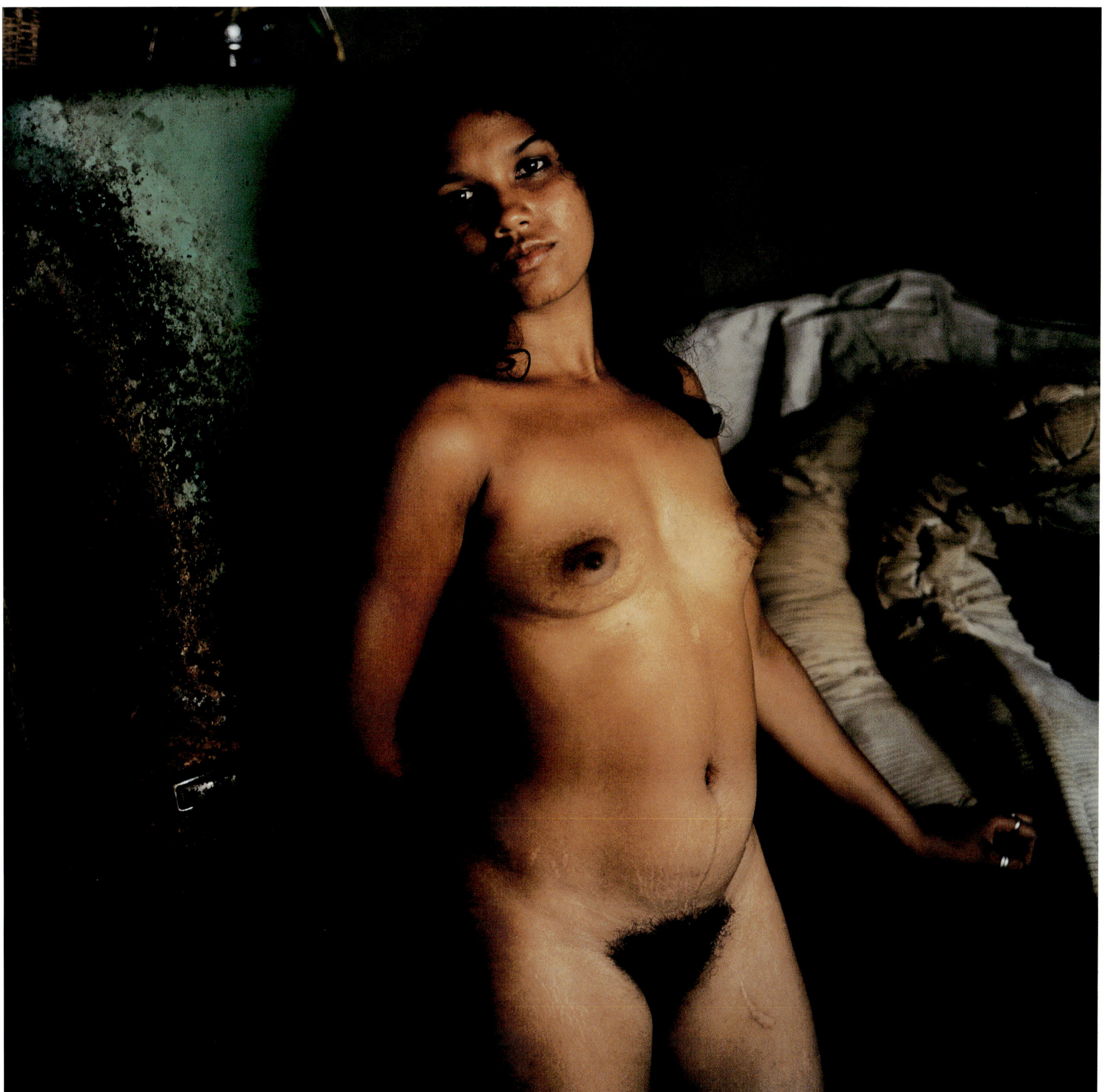

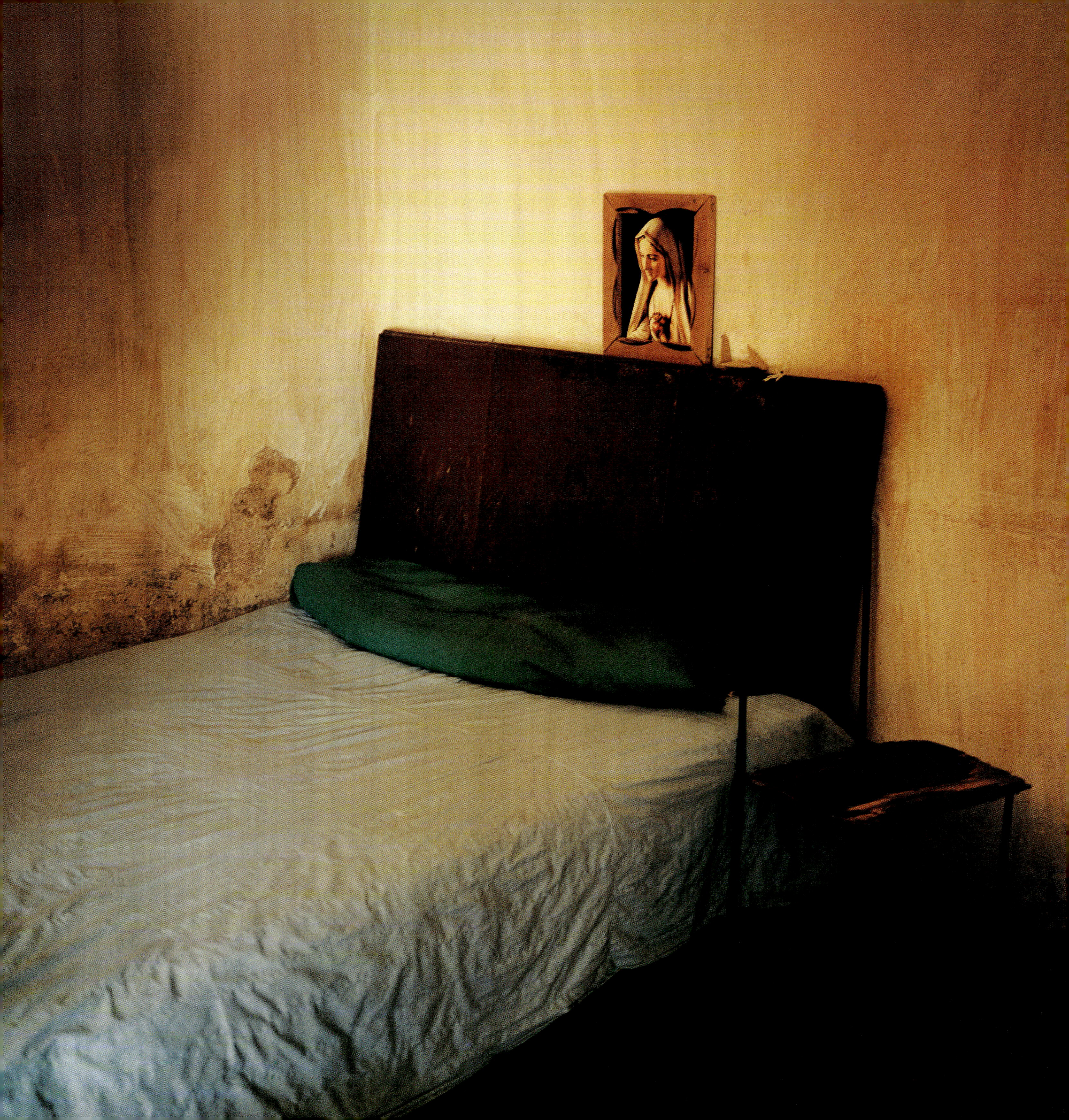

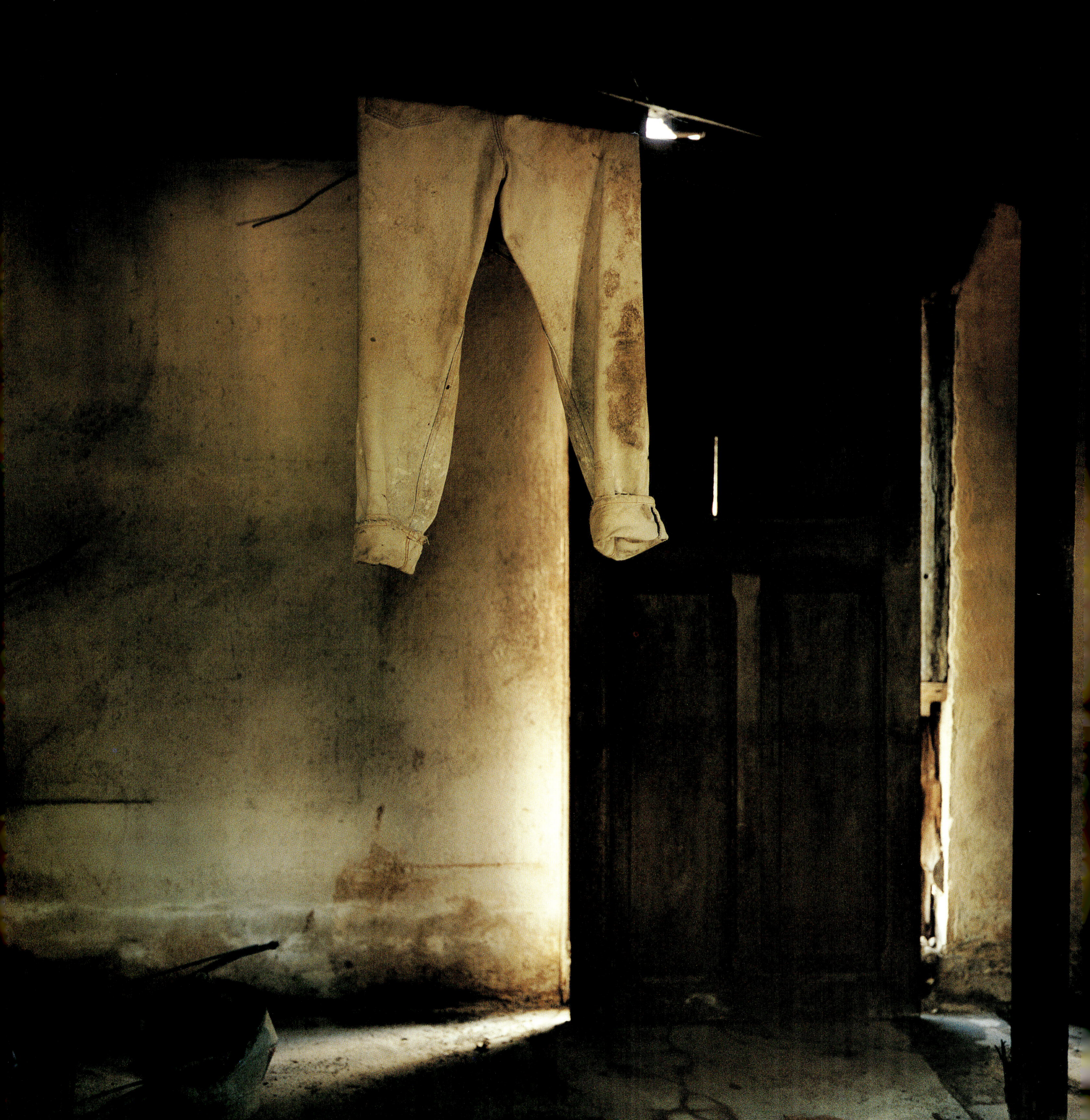

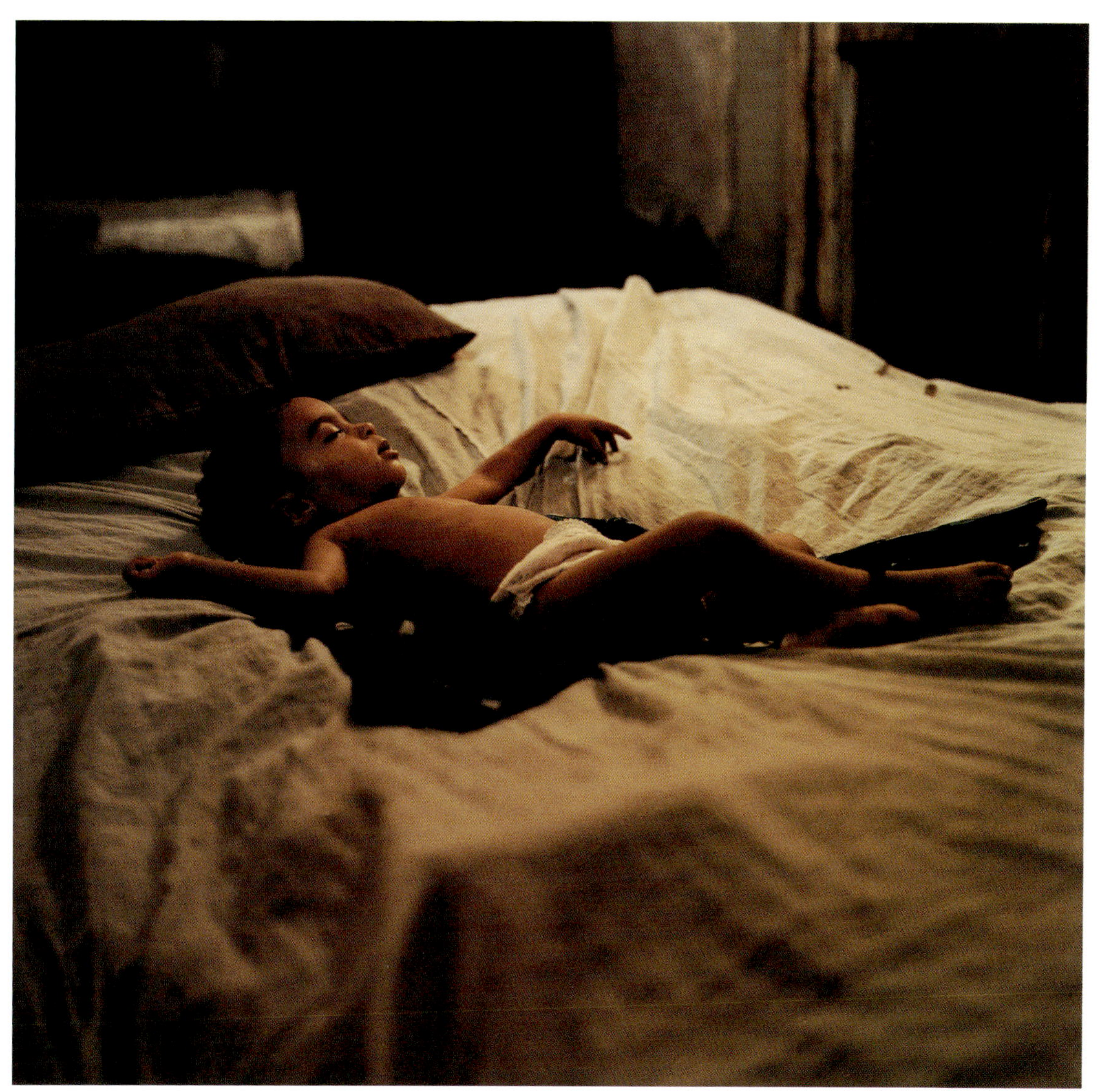

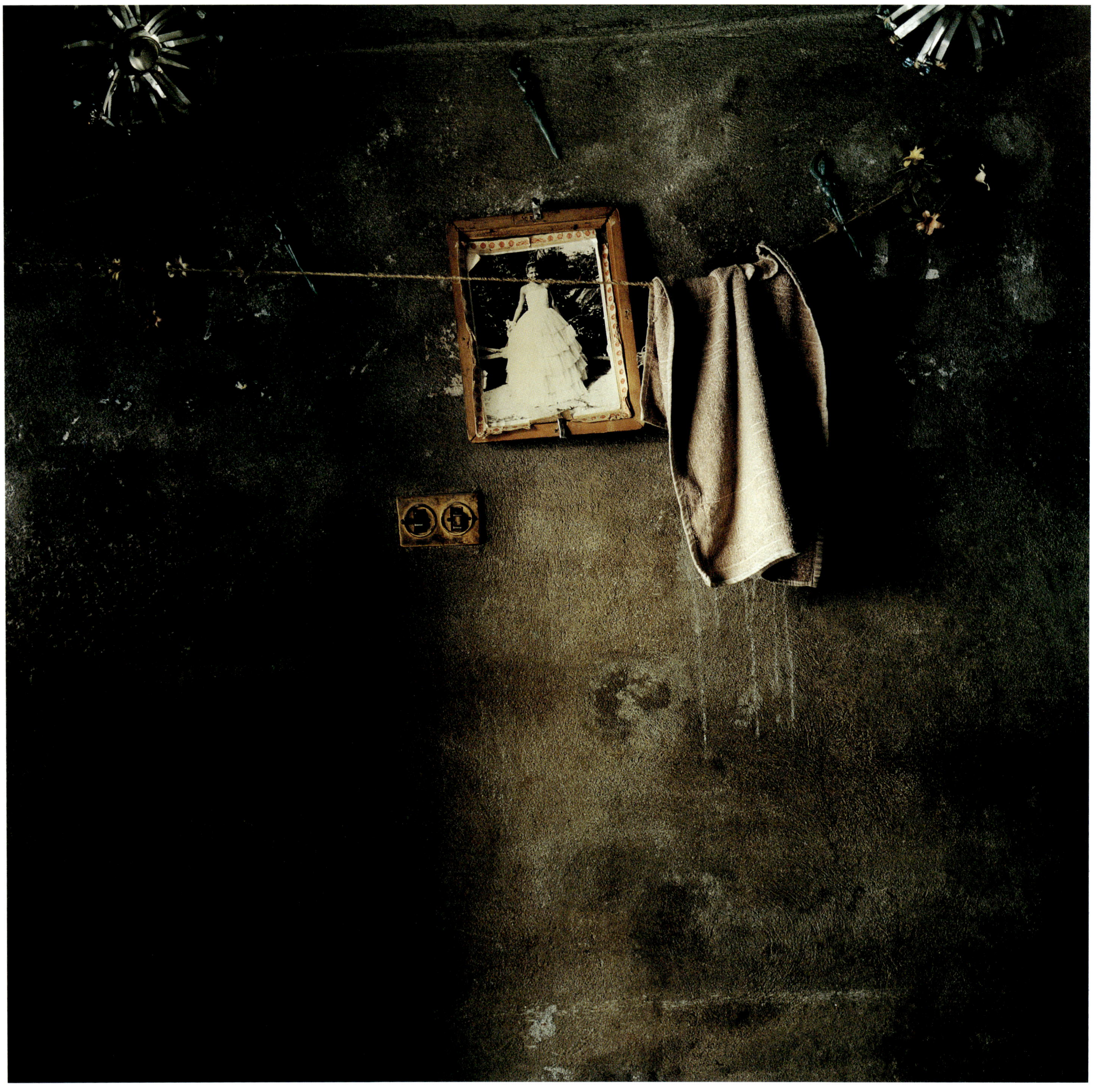

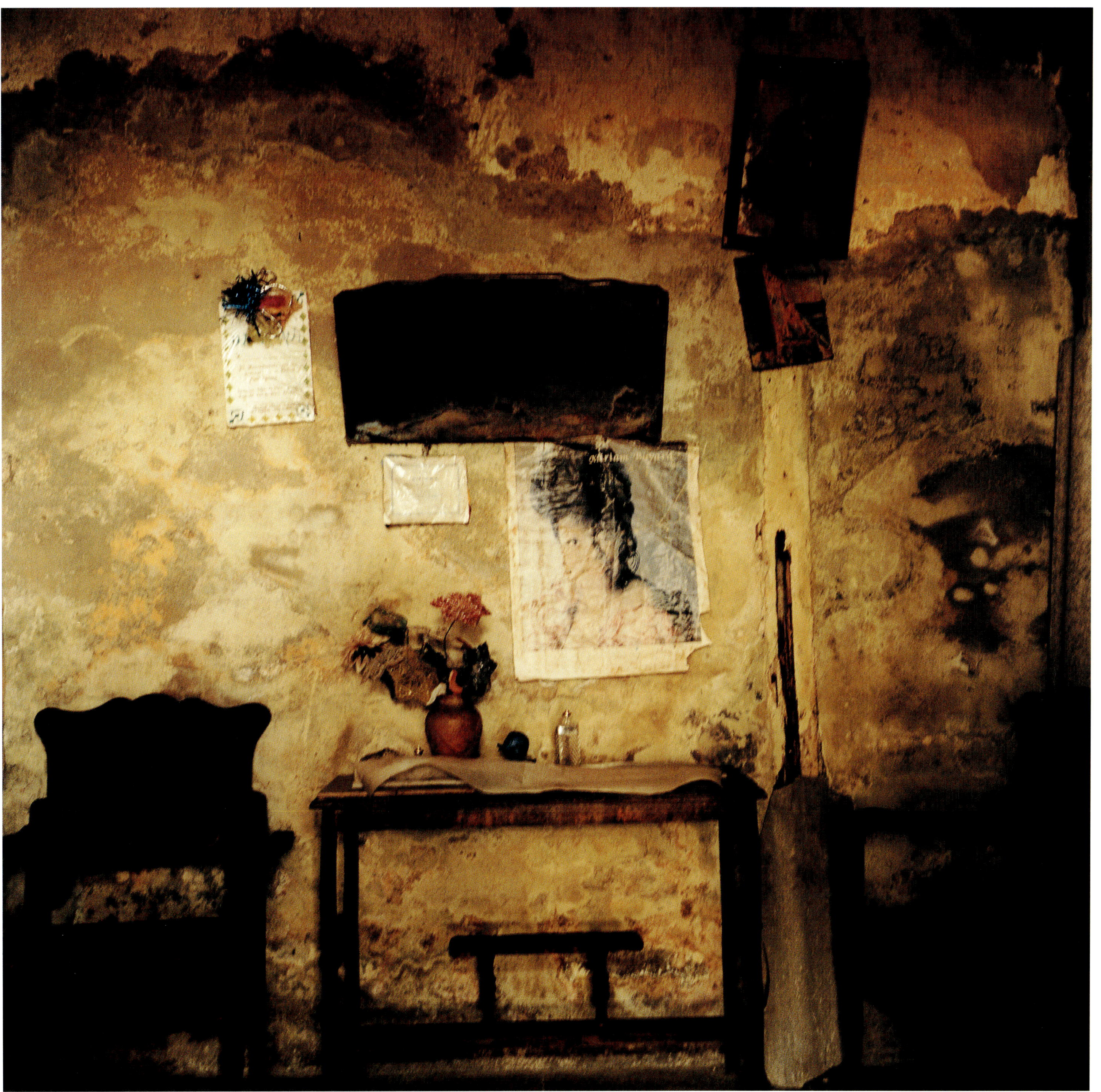

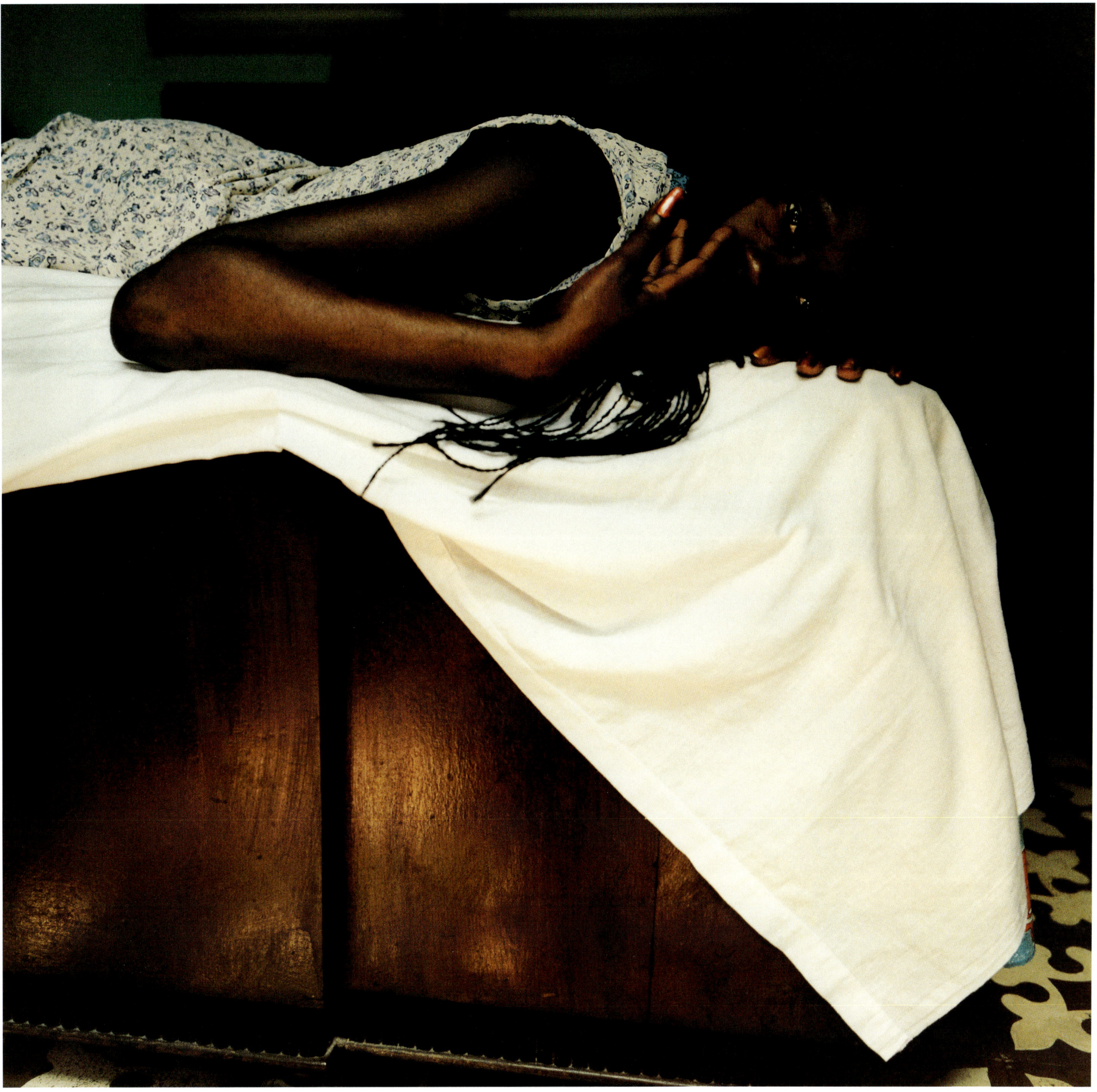

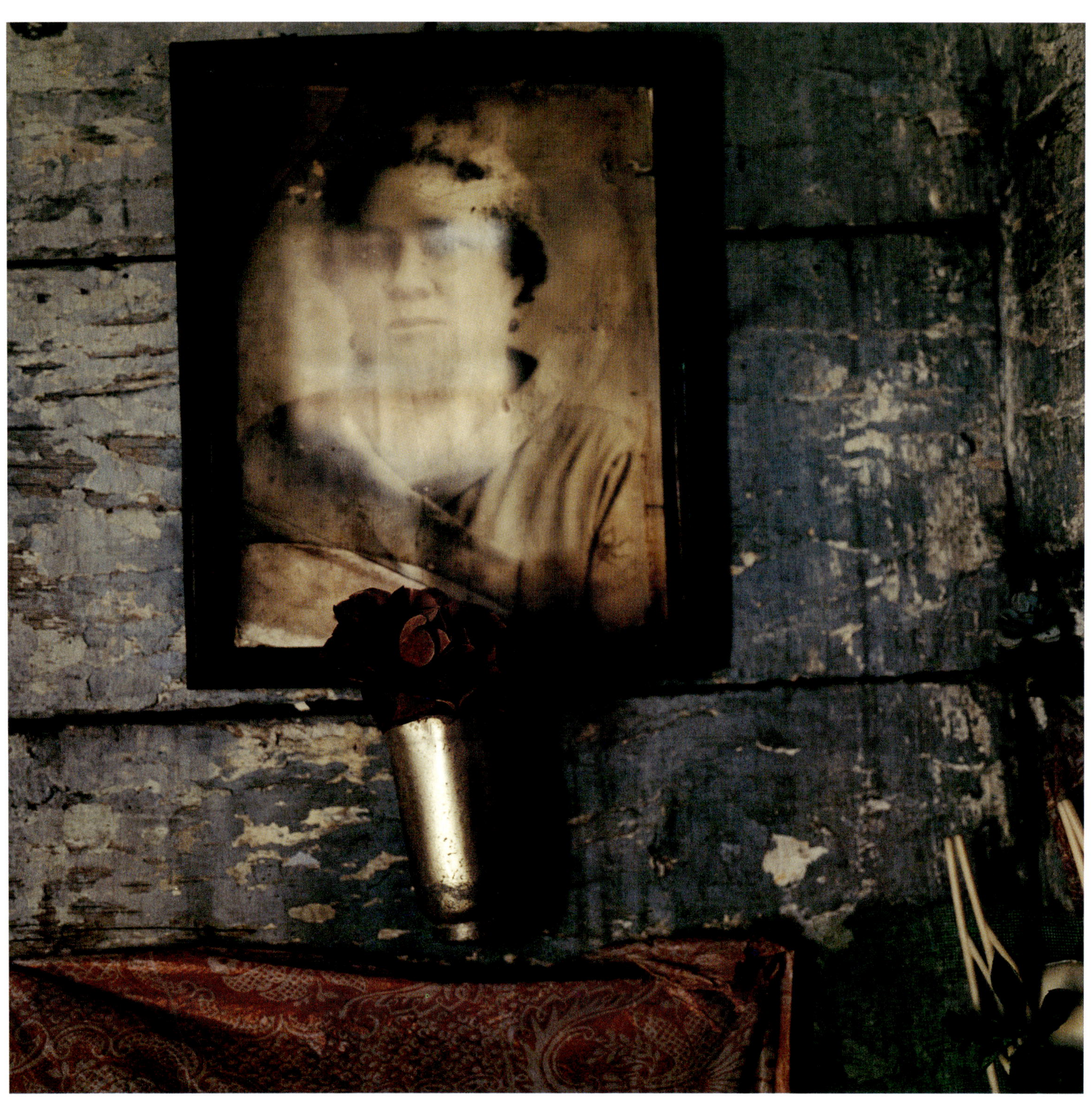

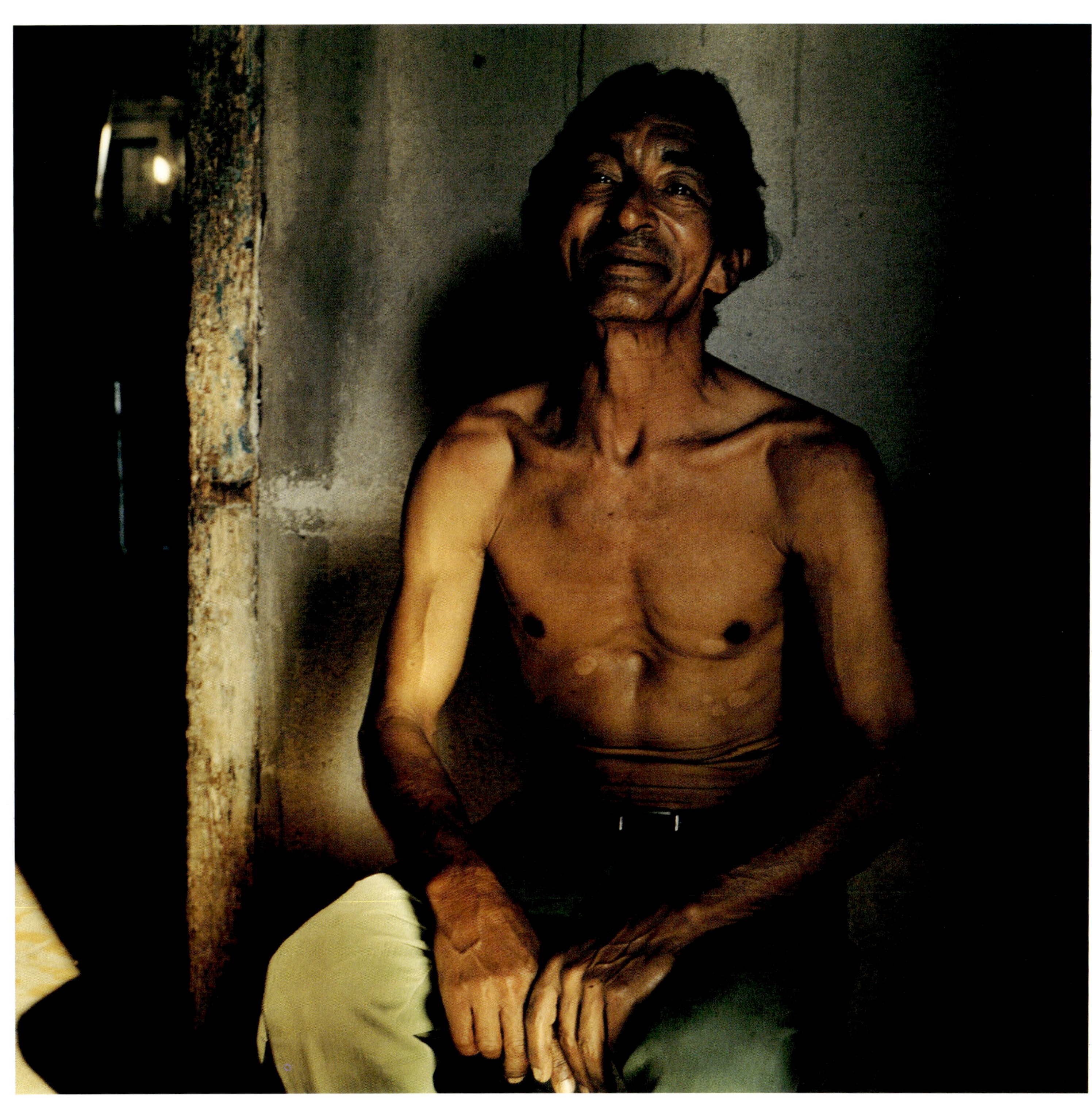

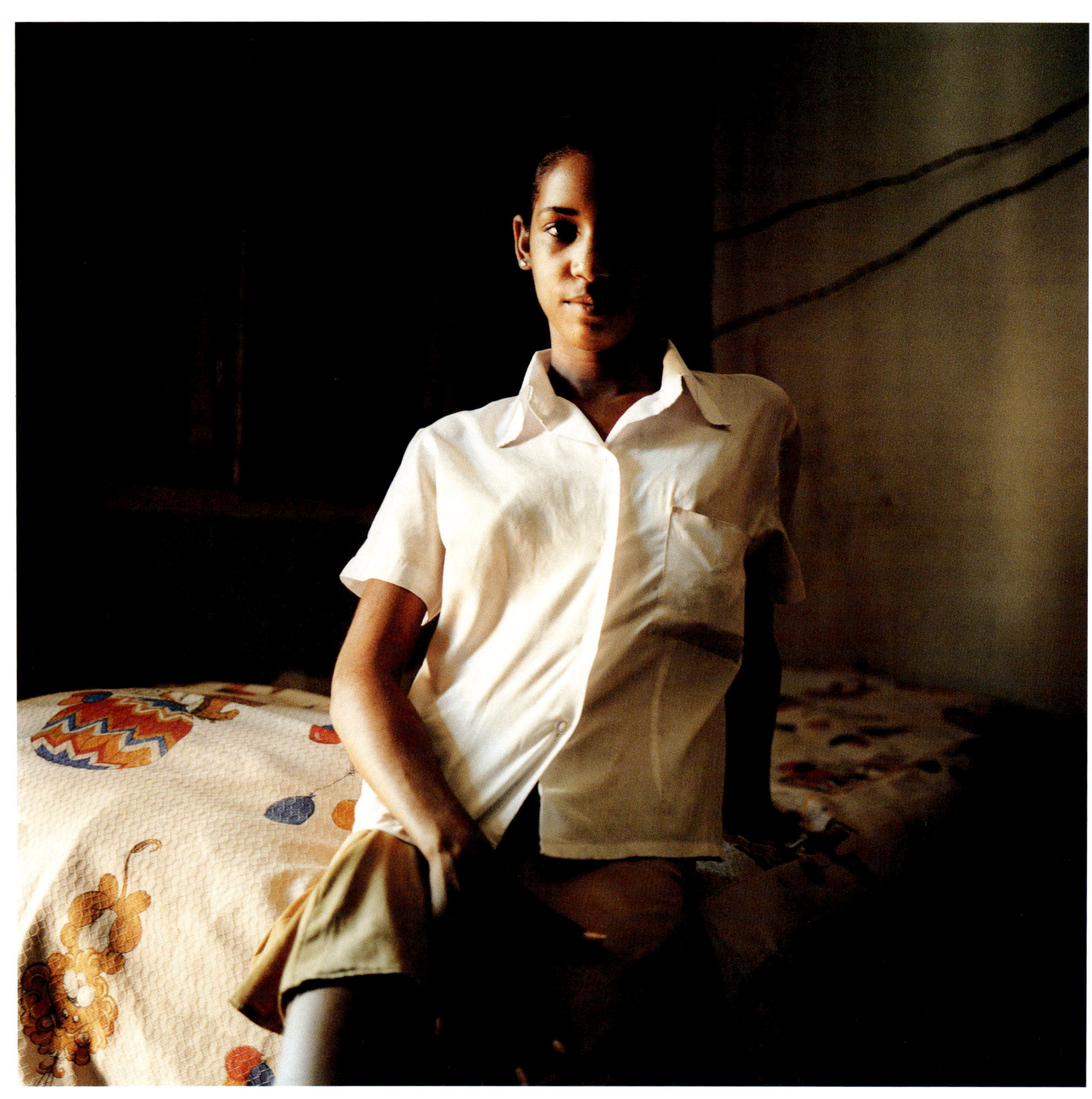

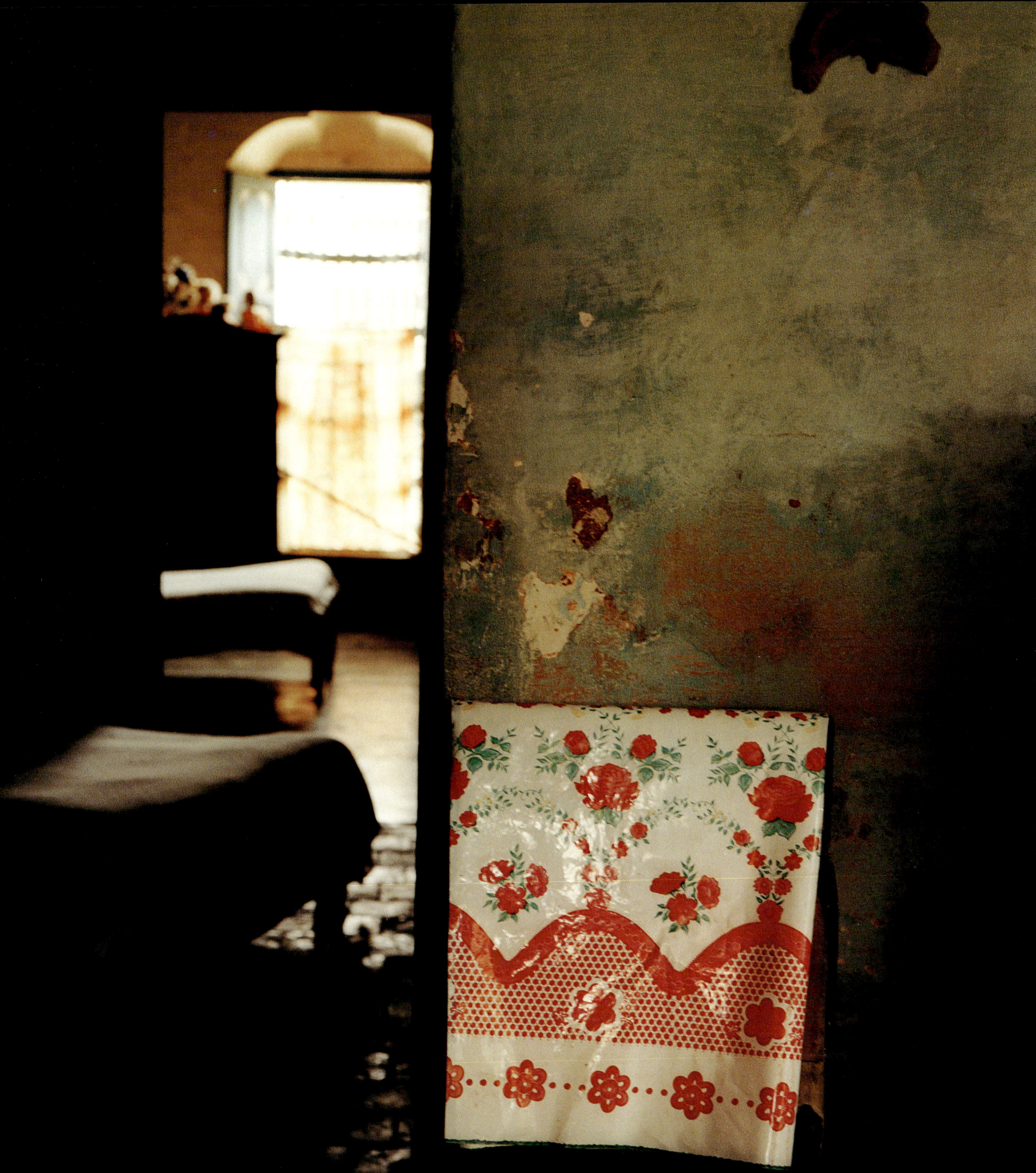

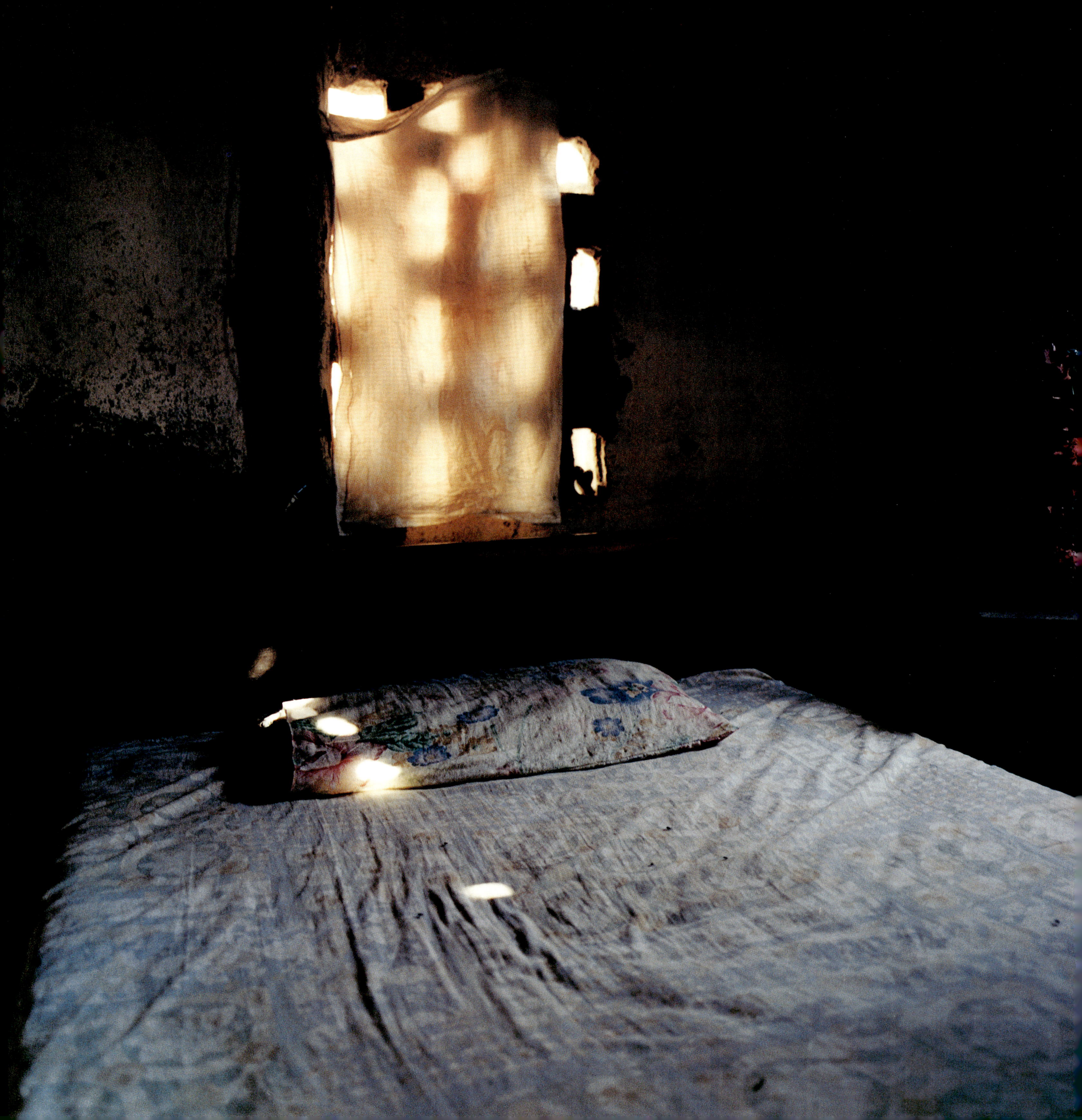

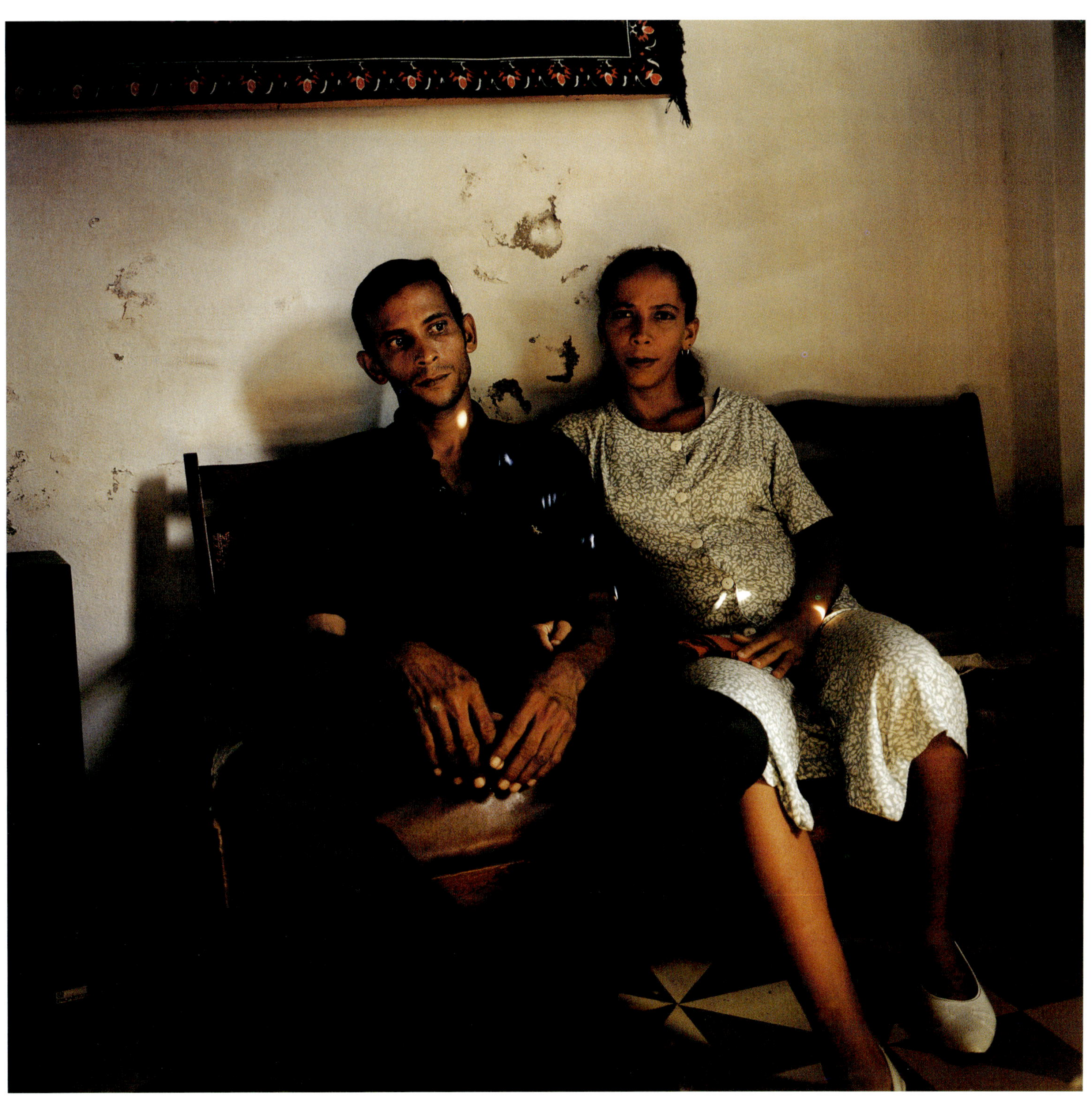

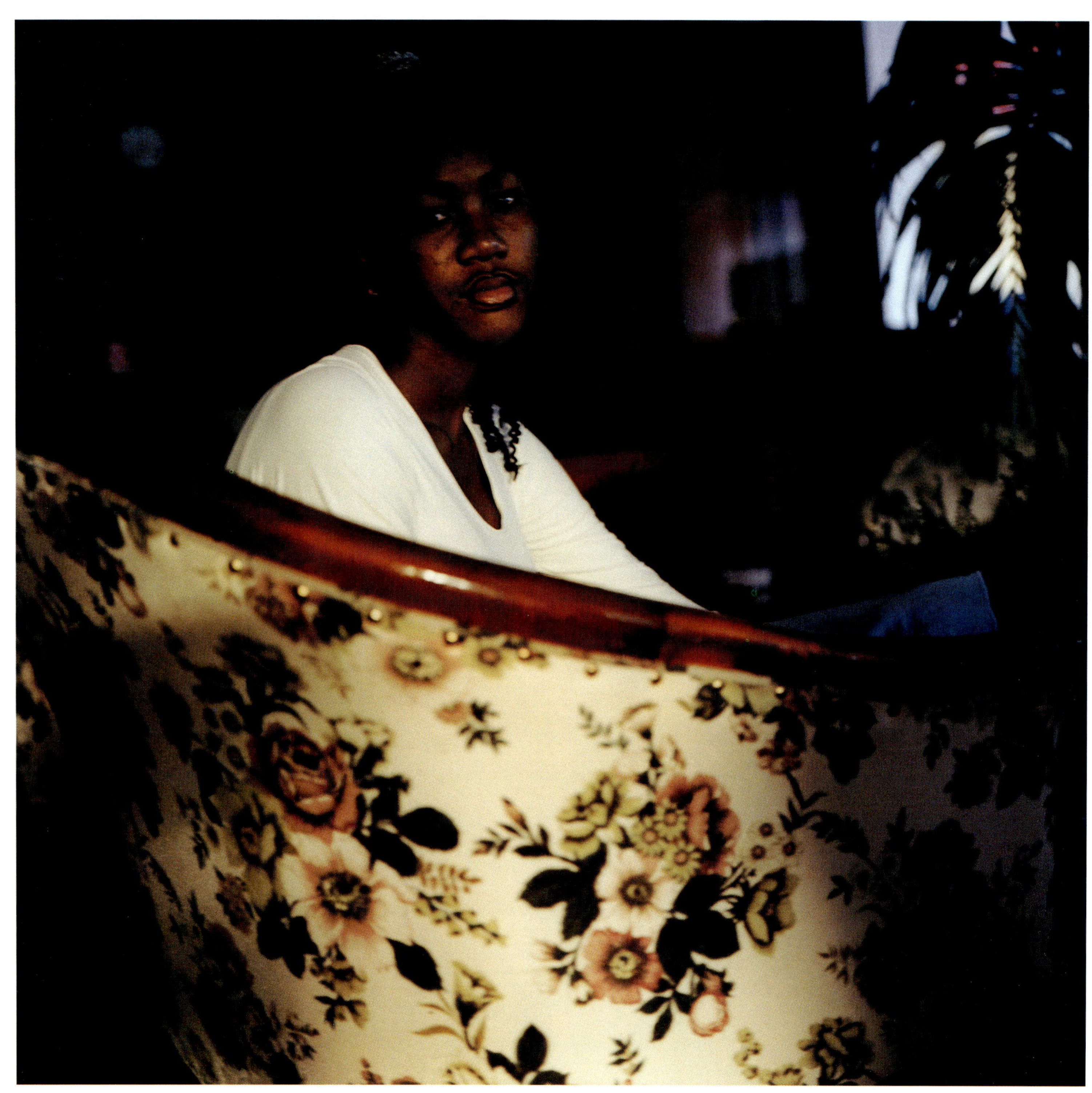

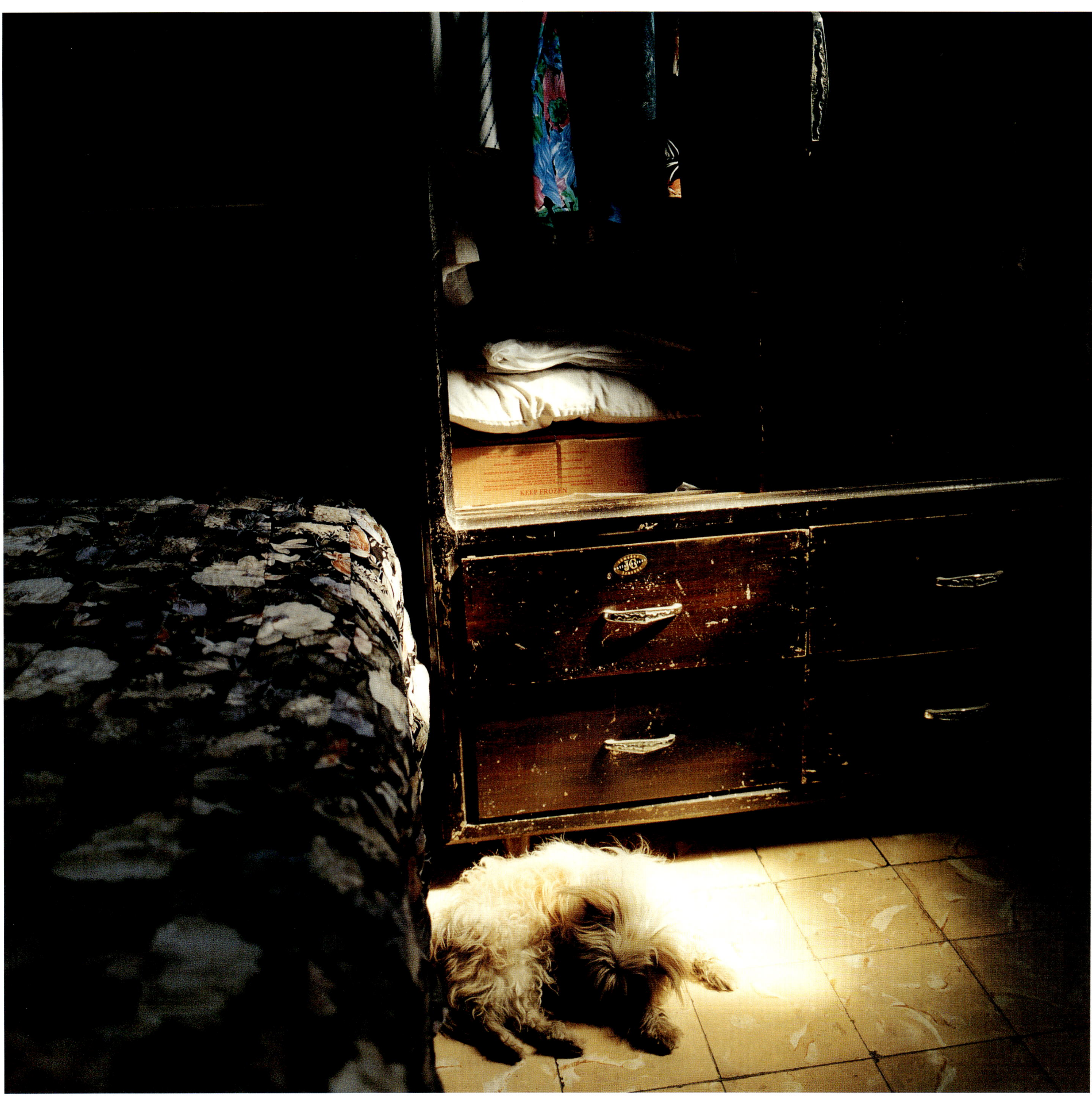

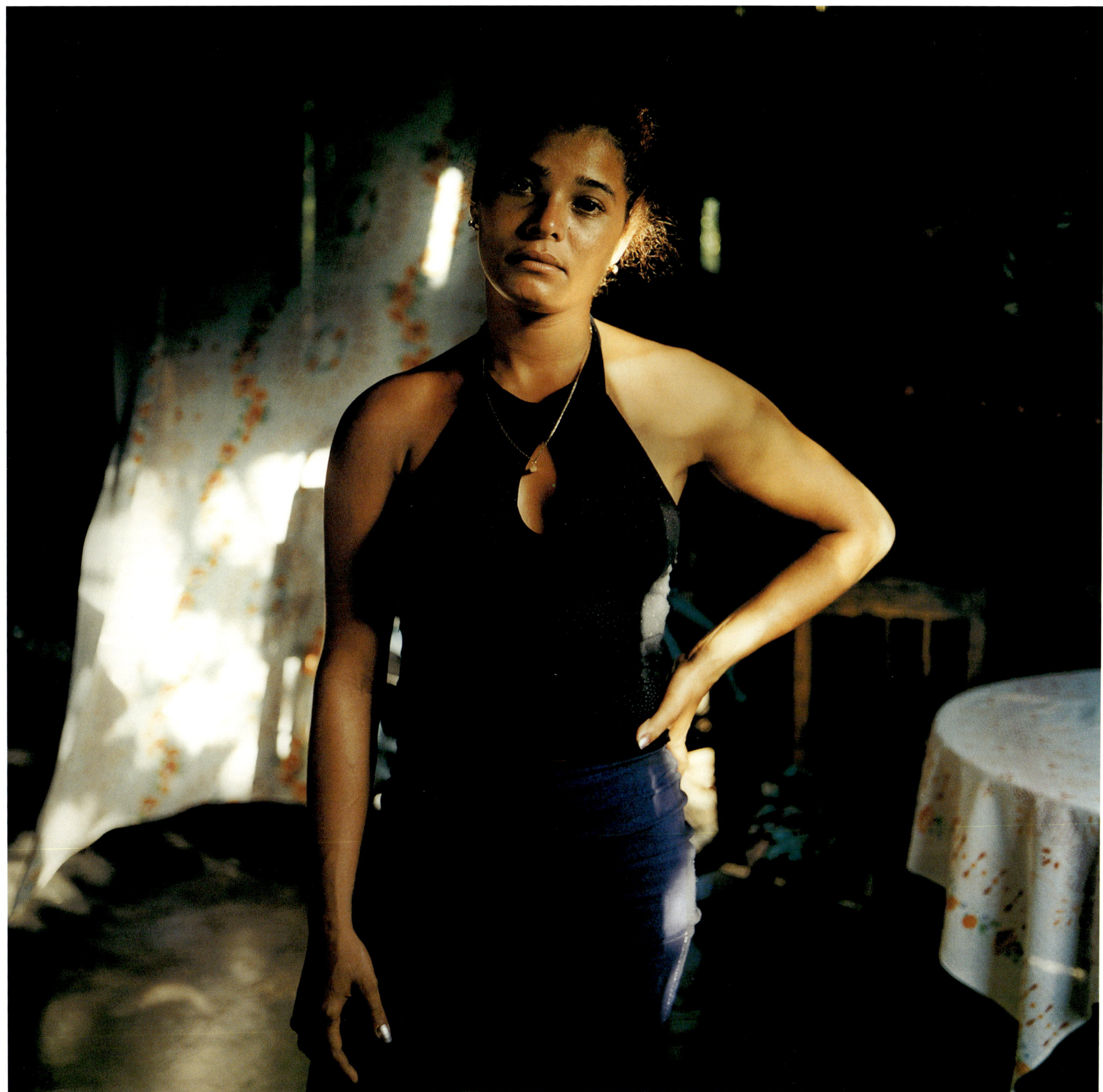

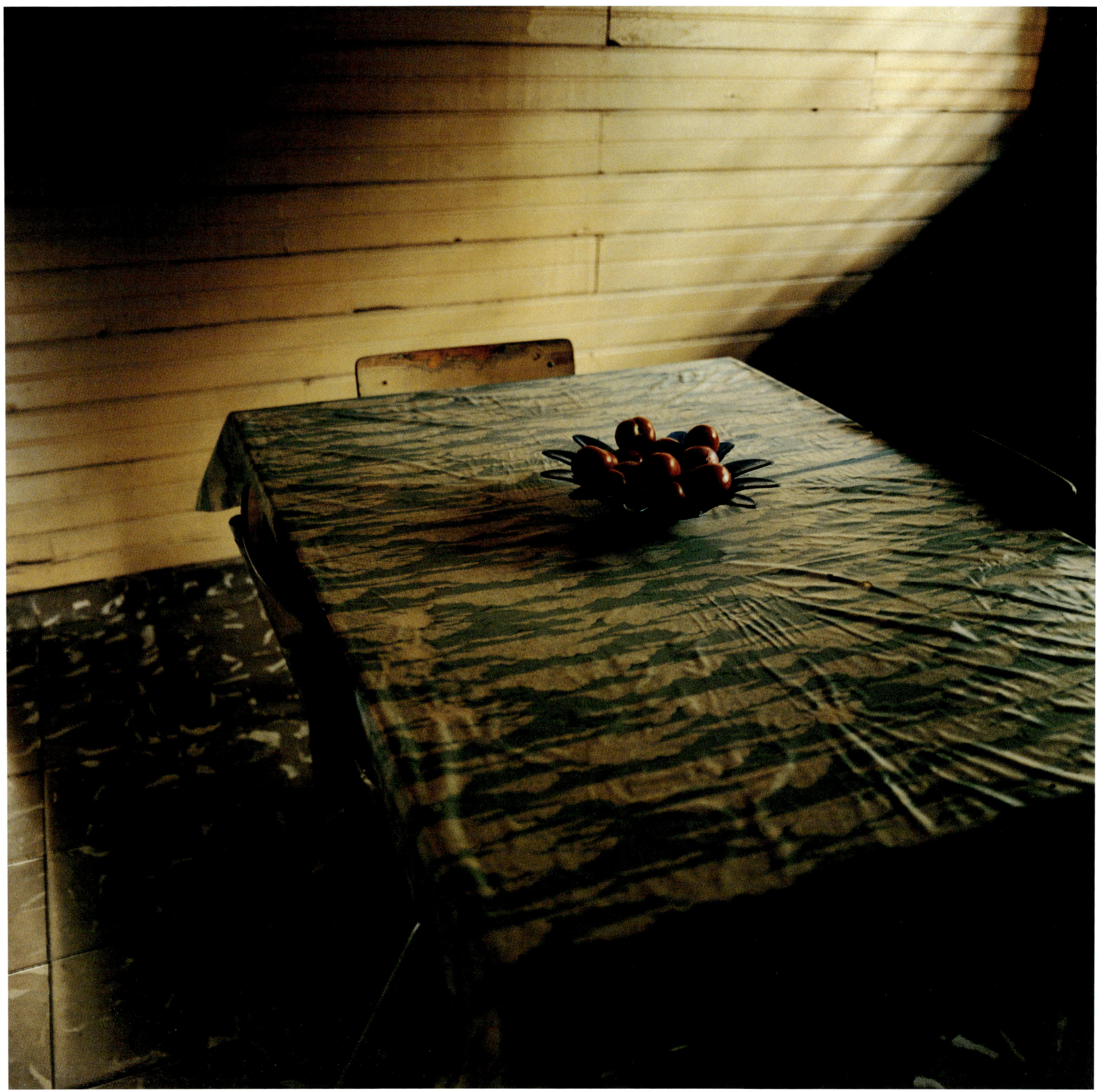

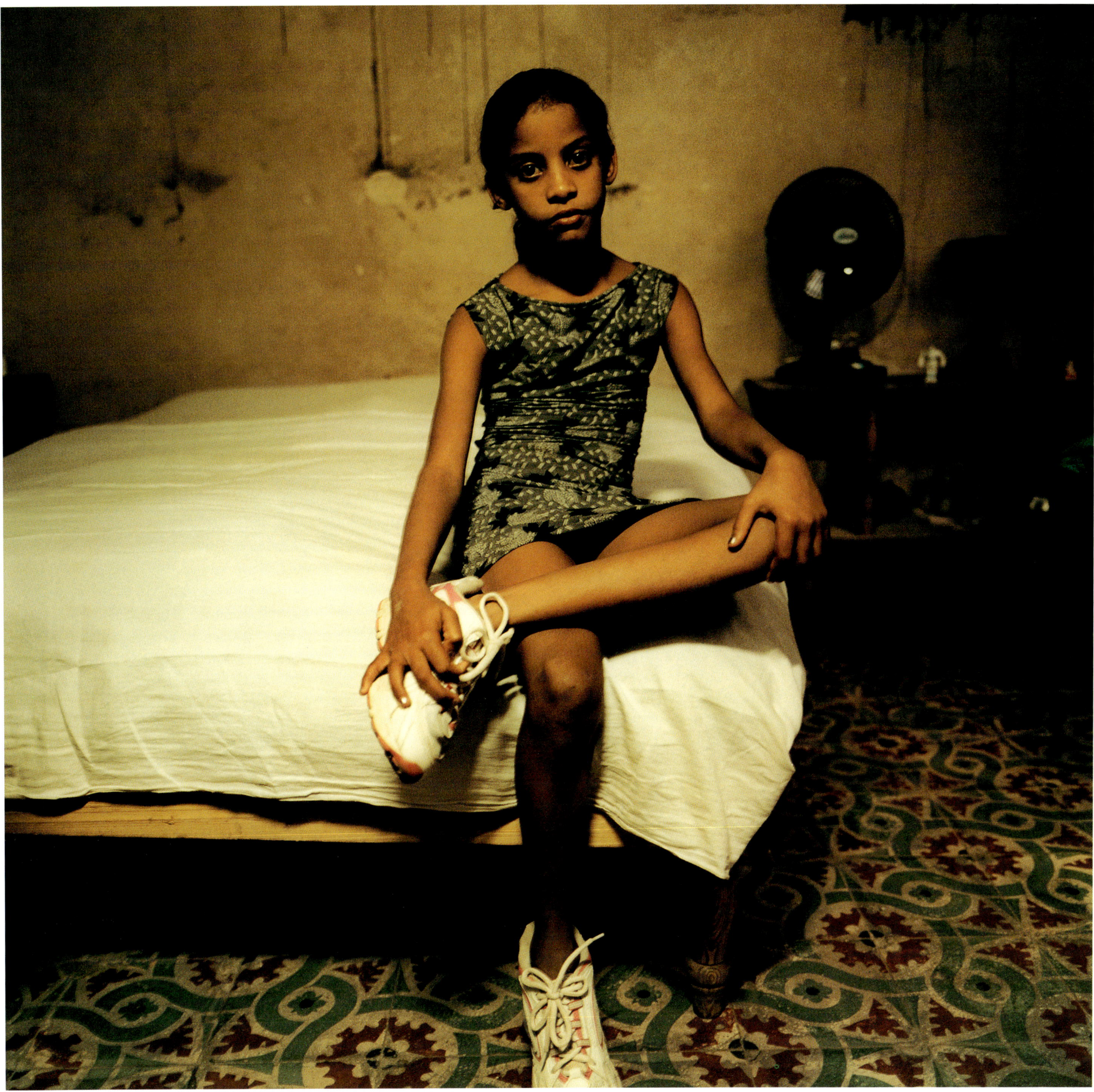

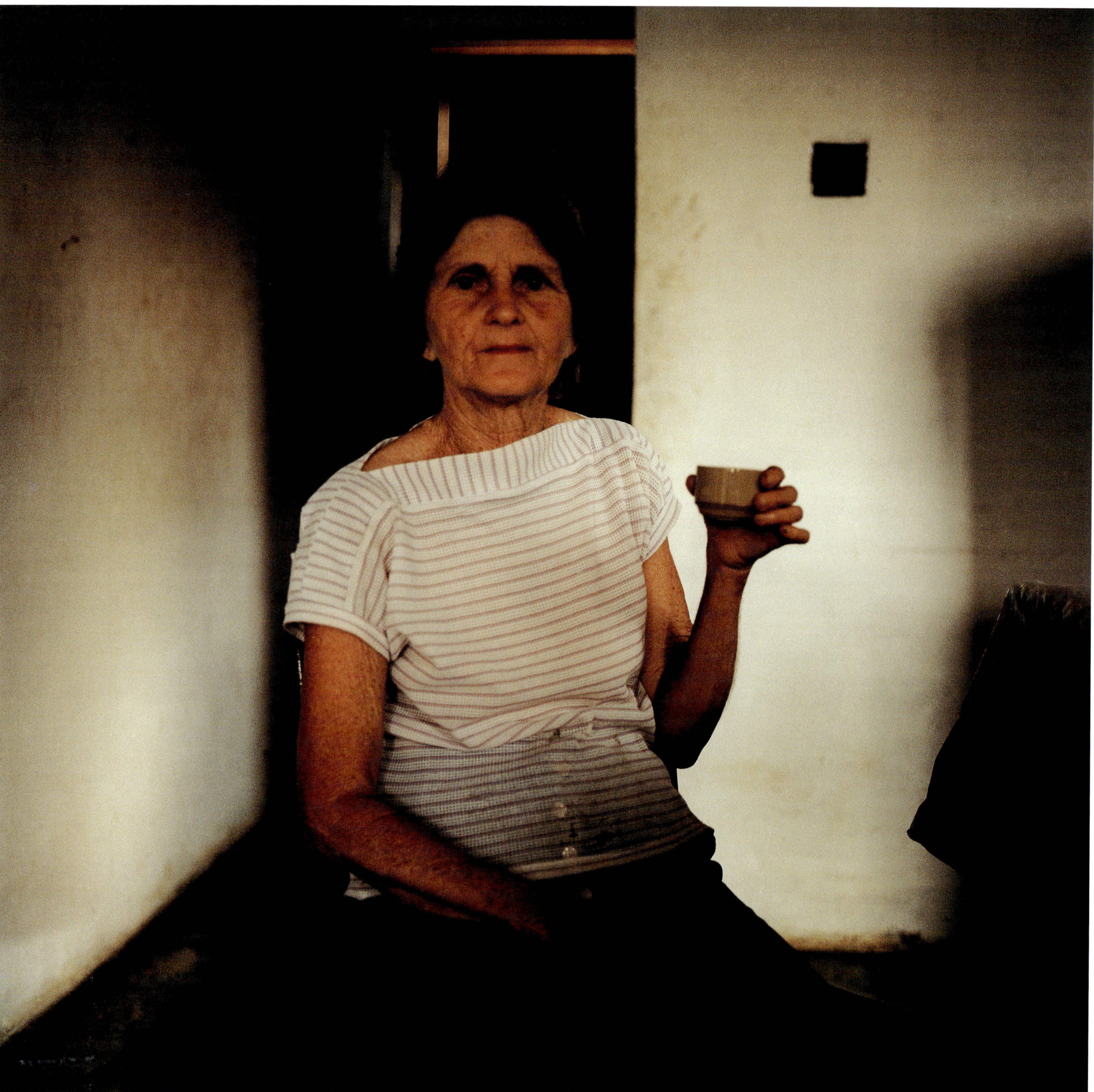

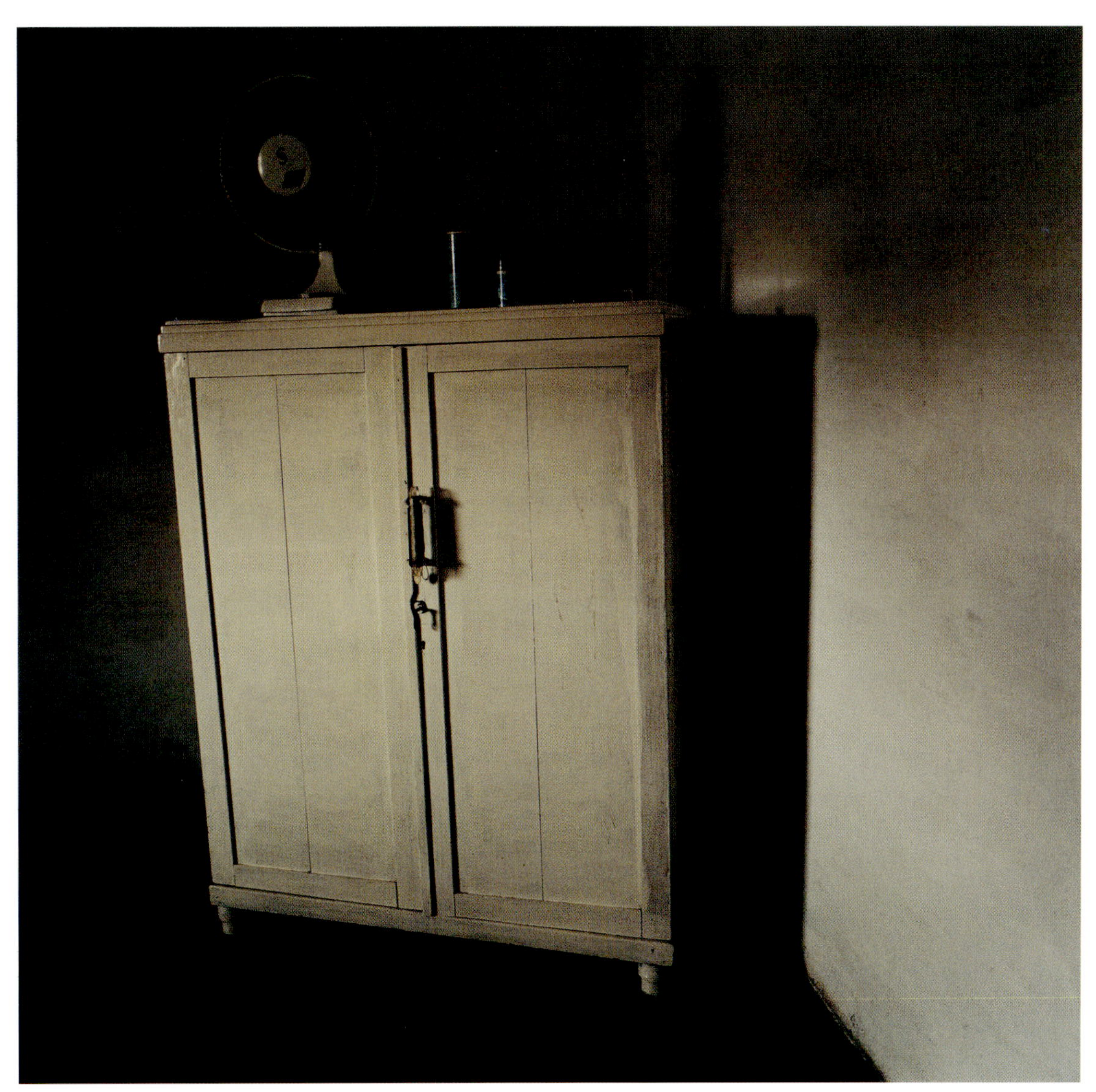

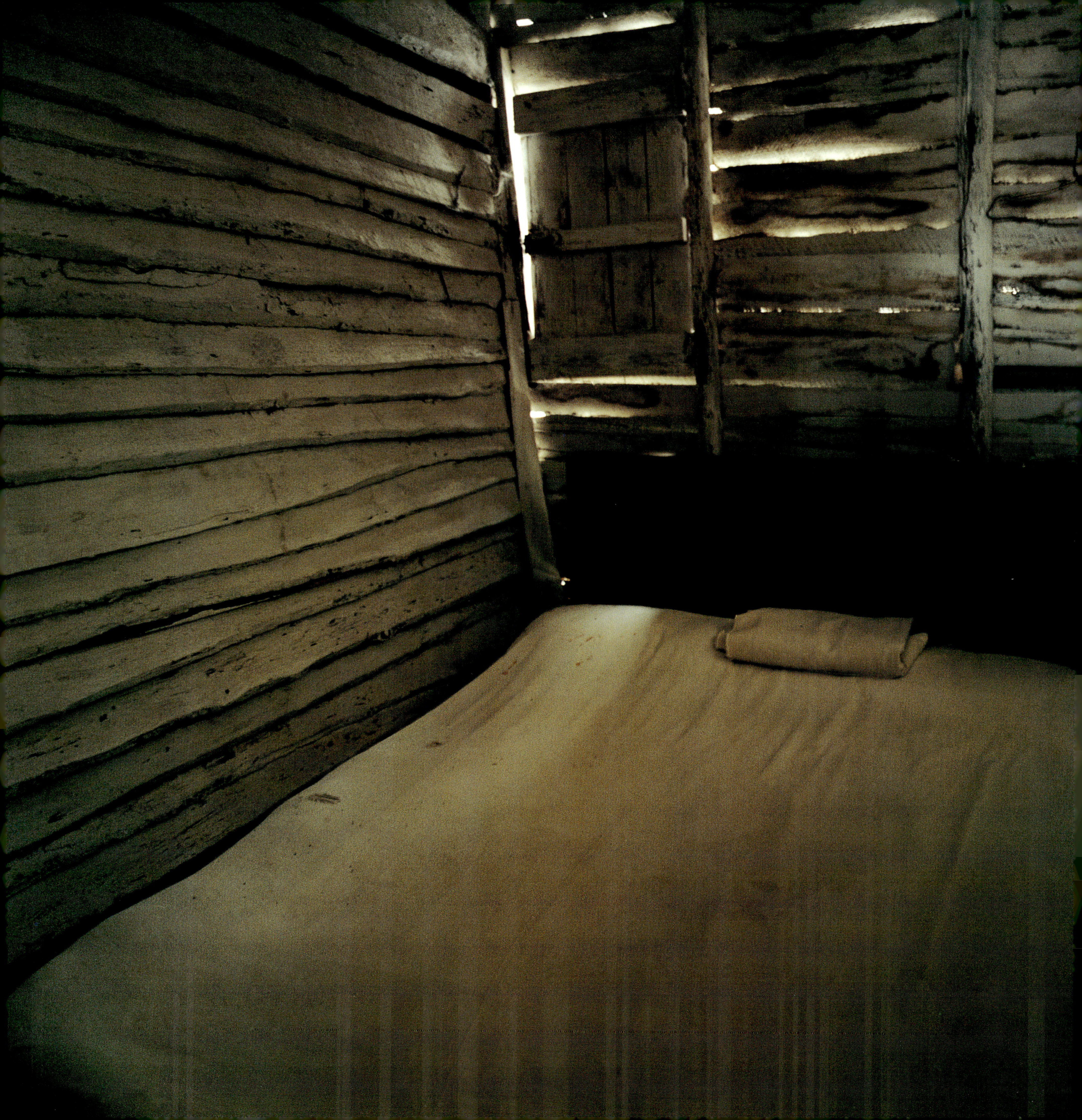

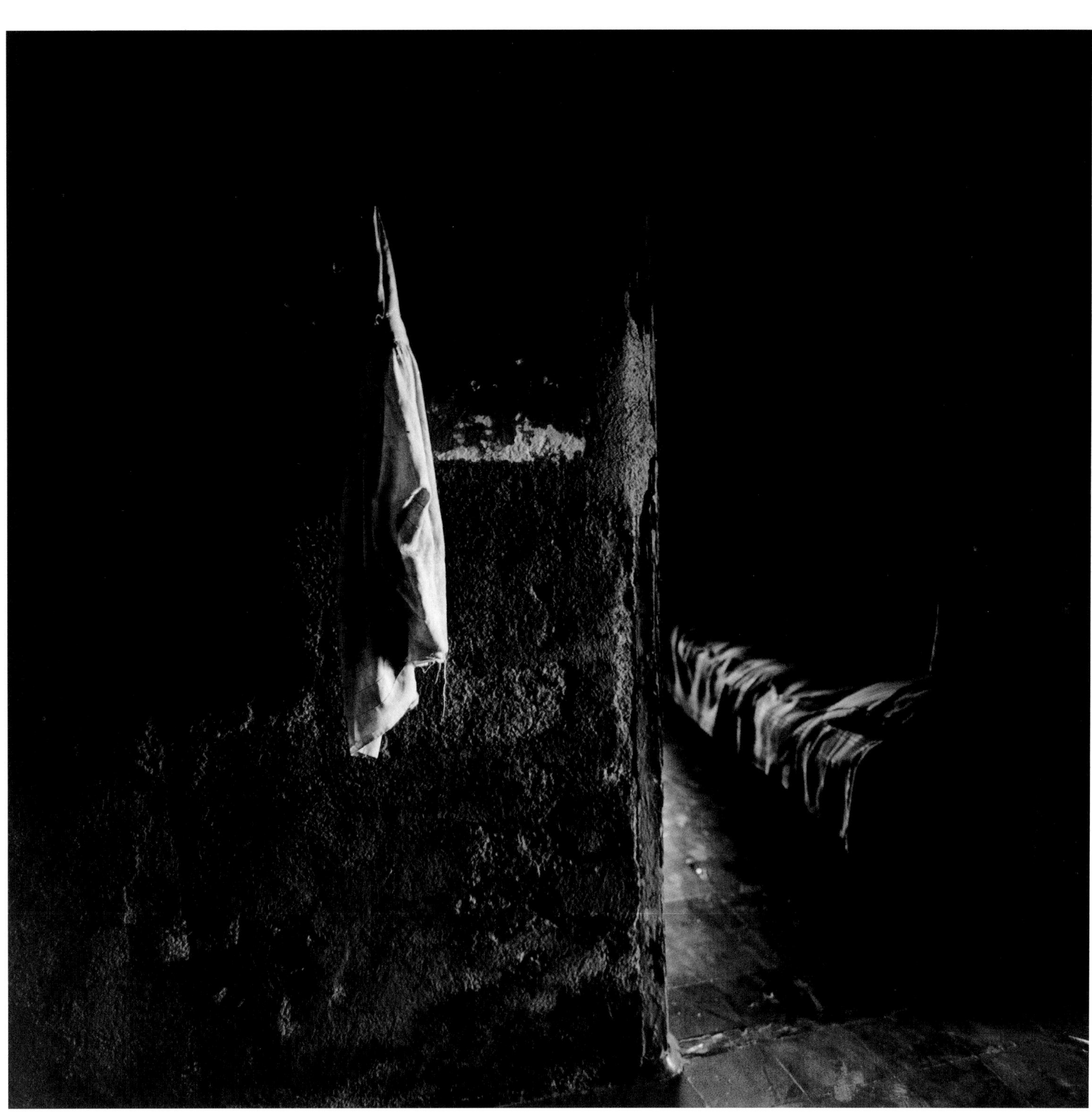

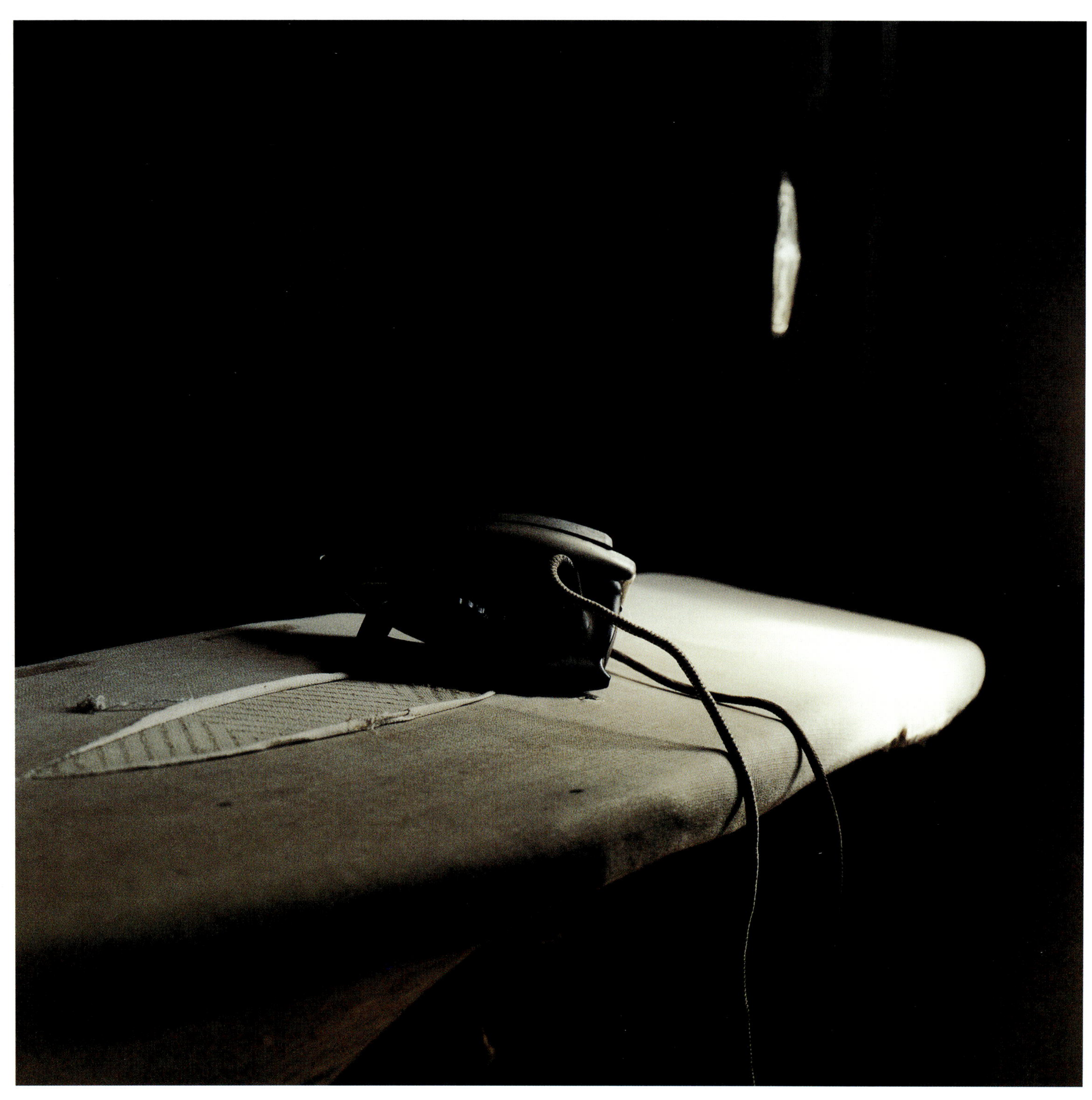

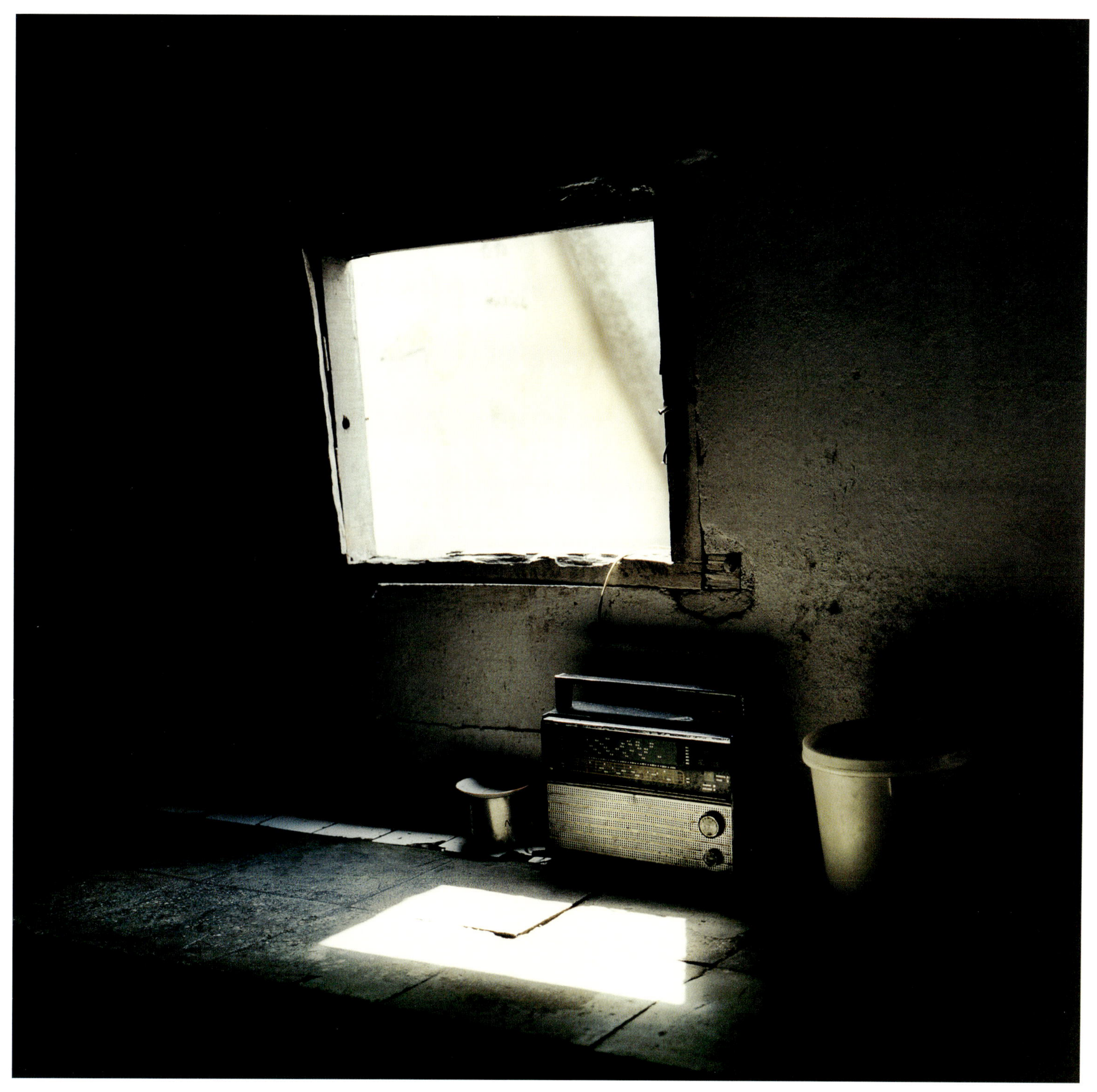

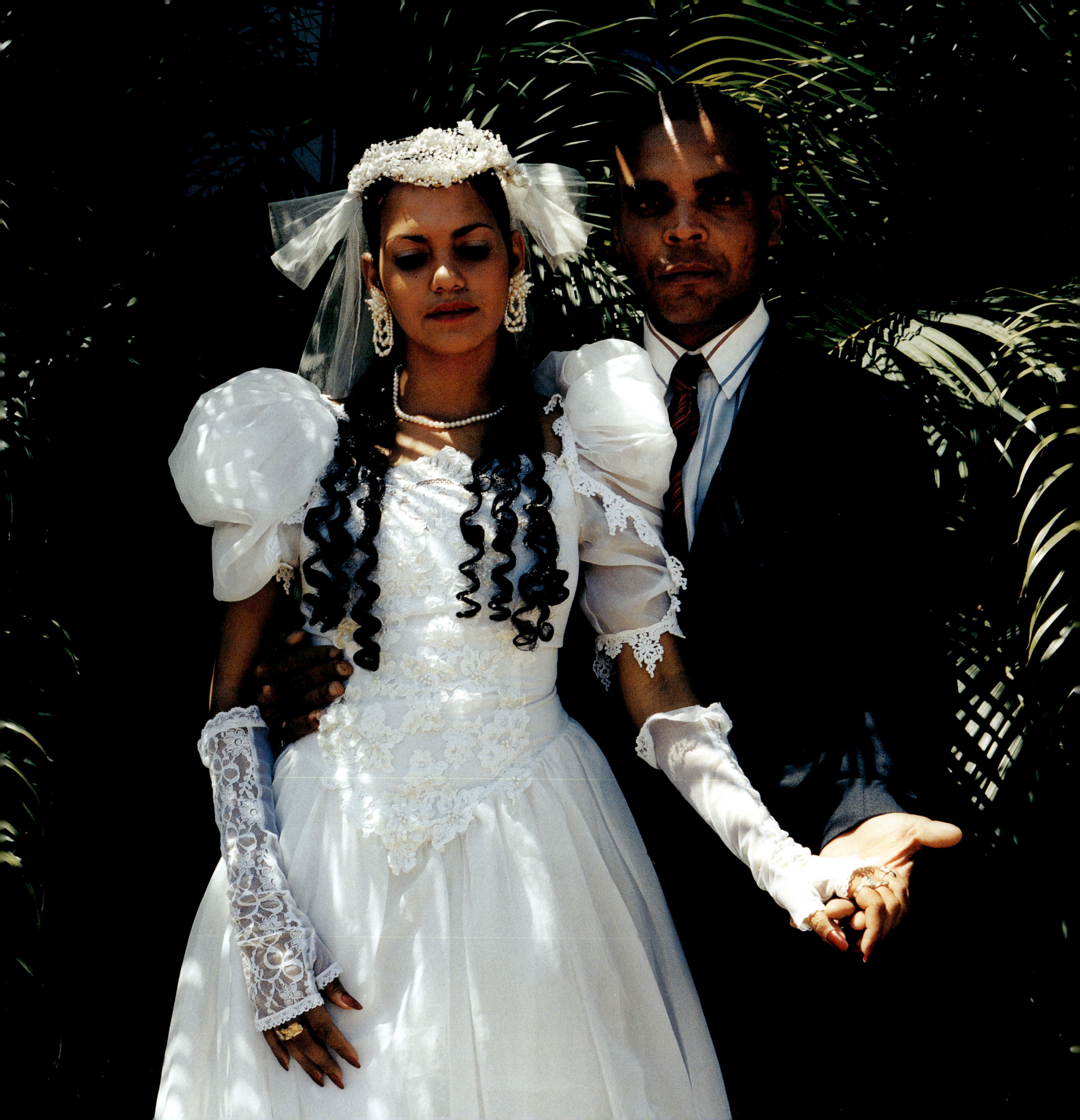

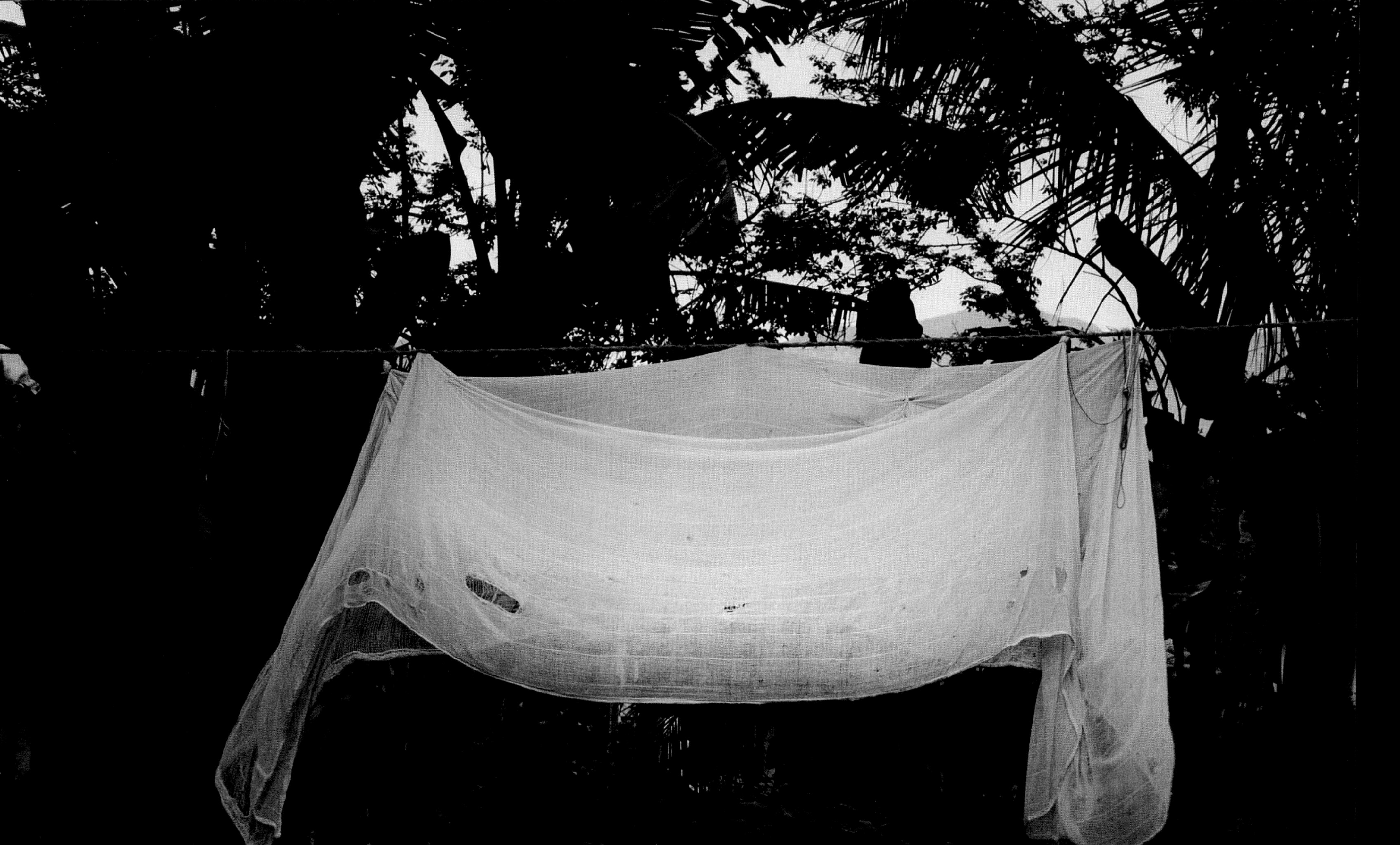

These pictures are taken in 'available light', and this is important. 'Available light' is a term often met with in photography, and it seems quite straightforward. However, it has ideological weight. It came into use during the 1920s and 1930s, and is often associated with the development of the Leica and Ermanox cameras. It is used with respect to documentary and reportage. It belongs to democratic and liberal cultures, and to their ethics. The idea is that 'available light' presents the subject in a natural light and in a natural habitat. Such pictures are trustworthy, and in addition they show respect for the subject. They imply that the subject has his/her own space and place, a space which is inhabited.

Most 'available light' pictures also show the subject as living in darkness, and some of these photographs make that point... two girls, for example, seated in a shadowy interior in a village outside Manzanillo. The sitter emerges from darkness, and is picked out by light. There are two useful terms here: emerging and gathering. These are terms from phenomenology, and both have an activist aspect; they stress being as a process. We are forced to look into the darkness to make out the figure, and light itself probes and explores the darkness... there are a number of instances amongst these Cuban portraits in which pieces of light seem to touch the subject. Phenomenology proposes that existence is not a fixity, and no more are we, but that we are always on the way, coming or going in conditions which are always changing.

There are other pictures taken in available light which are altogether more lucid, showing the sitter surrounded by personal or workplace objects. This second and different kind of photography suggests that we are again creatures of habitat, but also that we are artisans and collectors of things... we live, that is to say, in made environments... that we have assembled ourselves. Haris Kakarouhas's pictures are the 'emerging from darkness' type rather than the workshop variety. I said that this kind of

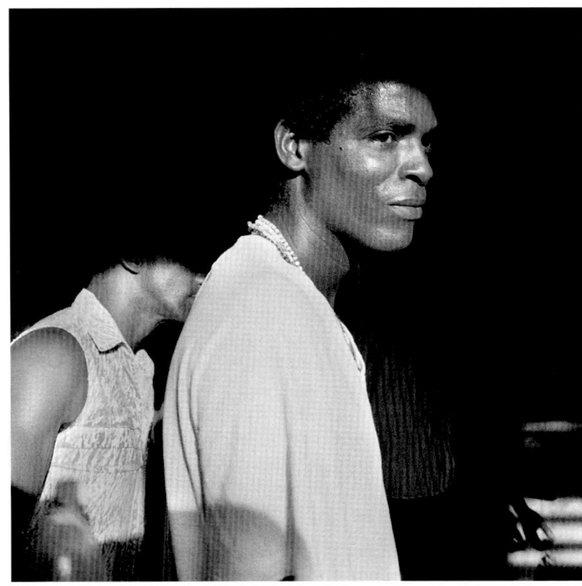

photography is democratic and liberal; this is because it associates people with private and with local spaces. You might also say that this kind of photography has an heroic dimension, for it emphasises individuality and effort... all this metaphorically, of course. The last well known photography of this kind was Bruce Davidson's *East 100th St.*, late 1970s, which shows people who seem to have been encompassed by darkness or assimilated into it... a struggle which they seem on the point of losing. You might say that there is an age of heroic individualism in photography stretching from sometime in the 1920s until the late 1970s. August Sander, who was rediscovered in the 1960s, is a different sort of photographer in the sense that his individuals are social beings, more body than spirit. They are rich in social signs, clothes and pieces of the environment such as doorways and garden plants. Sander makes us into forensic observers, attentive to the way hats are worn and shoe-laces tied.

Haris Kakarouhas's pictures have relatively little to do with this kind of detailed observation; they suggest that each portrait is a record of a meeting... an encounter. In Sander's art the subject has been envisaged as an object or as a specimen for analysis. Diane Arbus suggests that her subjects are open to specimen readings but that there is something awkward or inhuman and alienating about this. In Haris Kakarouhas's pictures there are individuals, but they are not the kind of individuals who appear in Sander's or in Arbus's or in Davidson's pictures. He stresses the importance of the encounter, and this, I think, makes them more postmodern. Earlier artists/photographers thought much more in terms of systems: Sander's is a very strongly articulated social system; Arbus's is a world of media and spectacle (Hollywood, patriotism, advertising, the Circus and so on); Davidson's is a social struggle scenario at a time of Civil Rights agitation, but in the postmodern era we are on our own, encountering people as they turn up... or as we randomly meet them.

One thing worth remarking here is that Haris Kakarouhas's are not street photographs. In street photography the transaction is quick and slight and the results are expressive and sometimes caricatural. He suggests in his pictures that the personal transactions have been more considered, that they are deeper, and even that he has put himself in a vulnerable position, entering the houses and spaces of other people. Peripatetic photography of the 1950s, for example, by Robert Frank and René Burri, implies that the photographer is a creature of the shadows, a sort of secret agent with his own agenda... an agenda which is in excess of the streets and their people. Who knows, for example, what Robert Frank's head was full of when he travelled in the U.S.A., for the pictures have all sorts of esoteric possibilities. What I am saying is that Frank, for all his keeping to the shadows, still had some idea about a privileged position (his own learning, imagination and fantasies). By comparison the pictures of Haris Kakarouhas are relatively selfless, devoted almost entirely to the sitter. Ascesis might be an operative term here, for it suggests self control and even self denial.

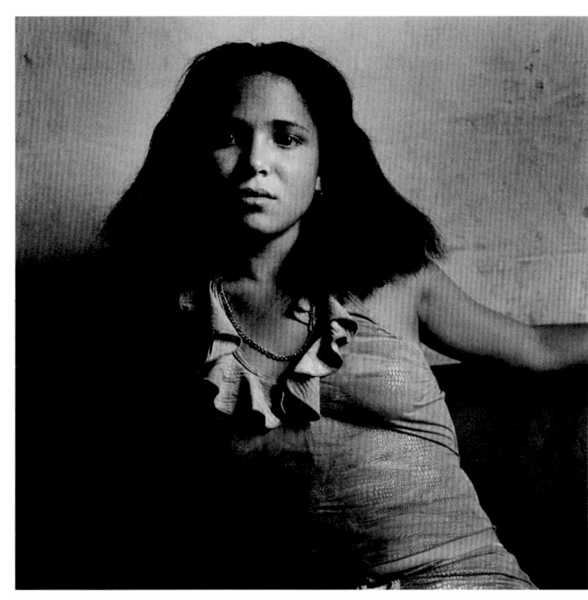

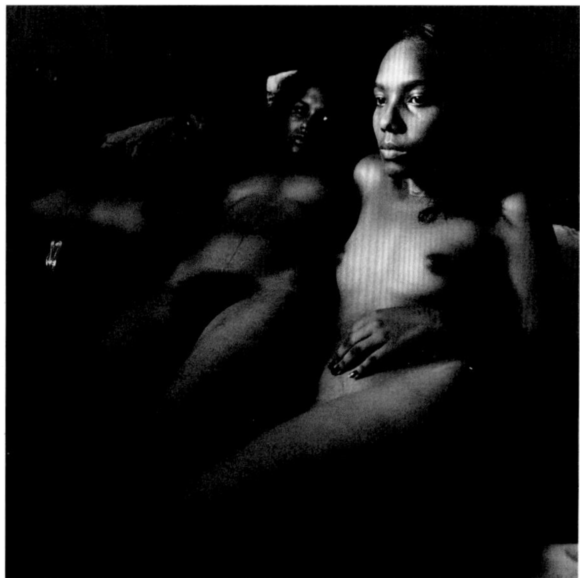

My argument with respect to postmodernism is that it is a reductivist moment or movement. Haris Kakarouhas fits in to this in so far as he takes pictures in which he lets The Other emerge, and that he is no more than an enabling device, or the provider of a space into which the picture/person enters. His contemporaries – I am thinking of the German, Thomas Ruff – apply their reductionism to the categories of art. Thus Ruff might take a portrait in which the conventional or expected attributes of personality and spirit do not enter. What Haris Kakarouhas has done is to remove any idea of himself as an imposing editor. It is as if he was saying 'I will start again and allow the world to speak for itself'.

I think that the contemporary bias is to show others as having quite separate lives and as being to some degree unassimilable into socially validated schemes... you might call this a super-liberalism or an ultra-liberal respect for The Other as mysterious. I am thinking also of the pictures by Annelies Strba (*Shades of Time*) which are about family and travels. She introduces other people, such as Linda and Sonja, who seem to be part of her life, and I wonder what right I have to look at such pictures. It is not

exactly a secret other world but it is apart from me, and somewhat indifferent to my looking at it. In former documentary and humanist photography it was crucial that I saw and sympathised, but this is no longer the case. Strba suggests, if anything, that some other people live in worlds of their own. It is also possible that some of Haris Kakarouhas's subjects live lives apart and that they appear only momentarily on your stage, and that there is a huge reservoir of otherness behind and beyond them... we can't bring them into our province in any way. A lot of Strba's pictures are quite ghostly, and look as if they have been taken from TV screens or home movies where everything has been enacted in slow motion.

By contrast Haris Kakarouhas's pictures are very site and personality-specific, and they are characterised by saturated colour. His pictures are certainly marked by saturated colour, in the way that Jan Van Eyck's religious paintings are... I would say that saturated colour points to desire... to 'the desire of the eyes'. The saturated colours, of draperies in particular, in his pictures supplement vision, for they place it with aroma and taste. Desire, in terms of appetite, has not been a feature of photography for some

time, and it is certainly worth remarking on. Saturated colour inheres in its objects and gives then an added presence. The portraits Haris Kakarouhas thinks of more as presences than as representations.

In his pictures he tries to integrate the colour into the chiaroscuro-defined form of the figure... I guess it makes them more present and more complete. The other thing saturated colour does is to make the picture more difficult to read or to interpret. I am assuming that the more one's senses are in play, sense of taste and touch, the less one's reasoning comes into it with all its interest in taxonomies and schemes of understanding. Modernist photography is in black and white and it is very much biased towards readings. His bias, by contrast is towards presence, and maybe this also explains his interest in domestic spaces and bedrooms – those many beds which he has photographed – where we exist in a purely physical sense. Mostly I associate colour with a kind of overall quality. It is not often presented in the kind of chiaroscuro settings which he prefers. Colour, as you see it in autochromes or in Seurat, is something like the 'colour of the world', a sort of drifting or omnipresent coloured state of being. By contrast he seems to try to intensify and to localise colour, and to show it too 'emerging from darkness'. You might say of it (his colour) that it enhances particular figures in particular spaces, and that its function is somehow to bring a halt to movement by filling out the instant, by making it full... by comparison to the emptiness or emptying out of self I was talking about before.

In general his project is radical in its selflessness. His long-term intention, is to bring the hidden inner self to the surface as a manifestation of qualities which are fundamentally human, bound neither by locality nor time, because as he insists the more deeply personal one becomes, the more he can communicate across boundaries with The Other.

Ian Jeffrey

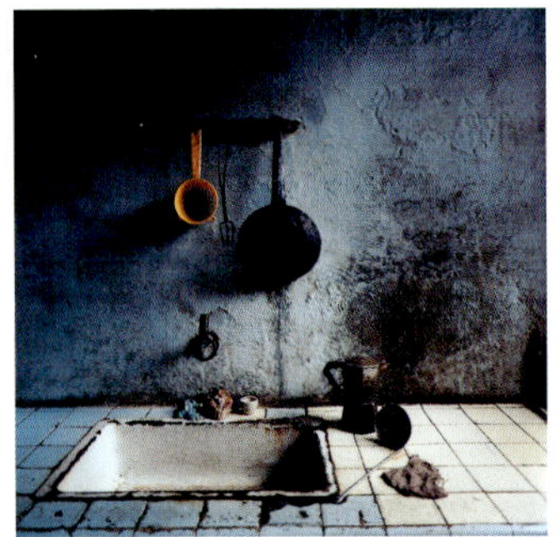

Manzanillo, Granma, June 2001

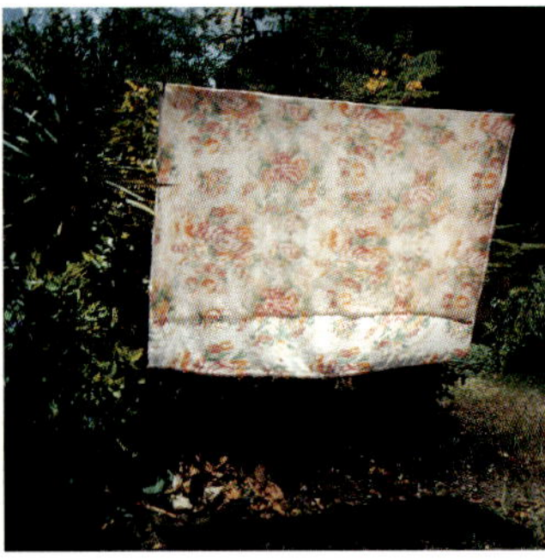

Baracoa, Guantanamo, July 2001

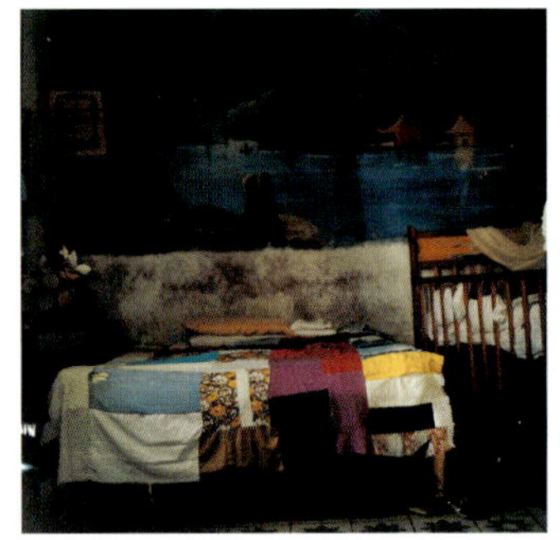

El Tivoli, Santiago de Cuba, June 2002

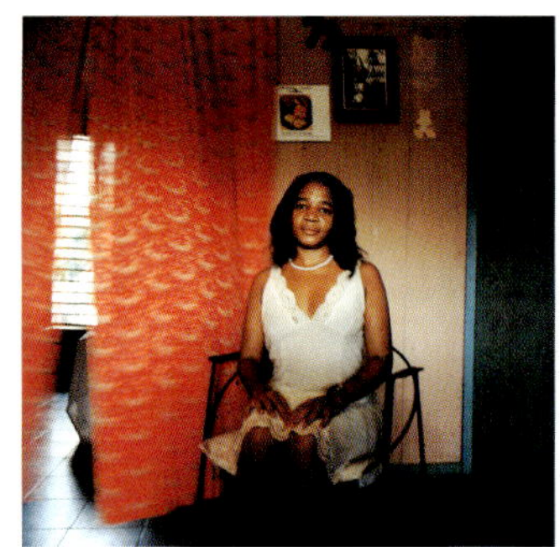

Yoanis Espinosa, Santiago de Cuba, May 2002

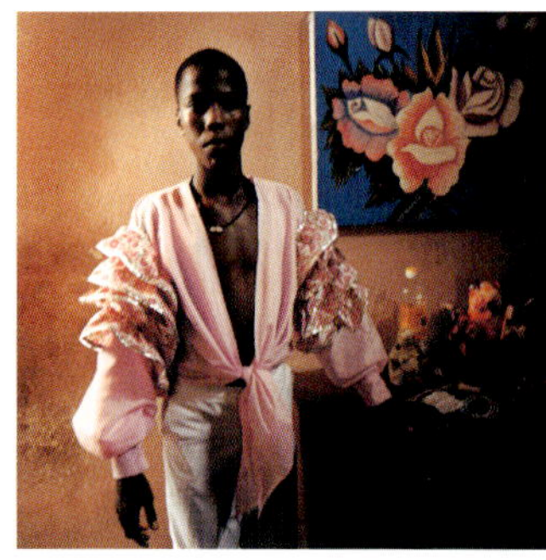

Gabriel, Los Olmos, Santiago de Cuba, July 2001

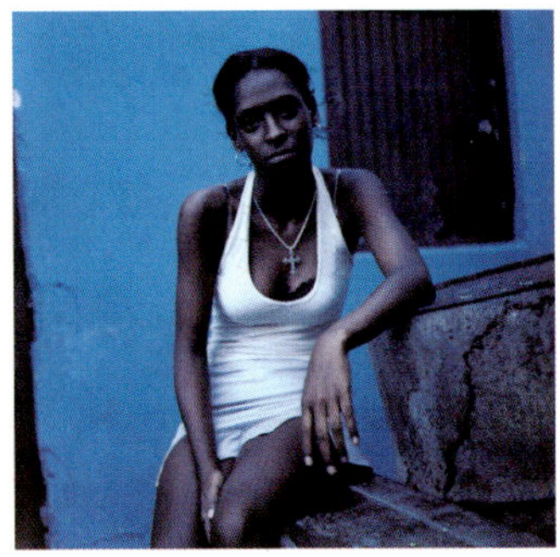

Maria Elena, El Tivoli, Santiago de Cuba, July 2001

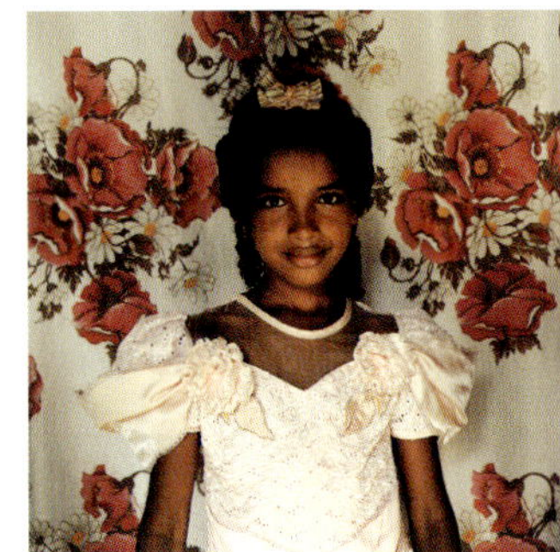

Yanisleidis Suarez, Municipal, Santiago de Cuba, May 2002

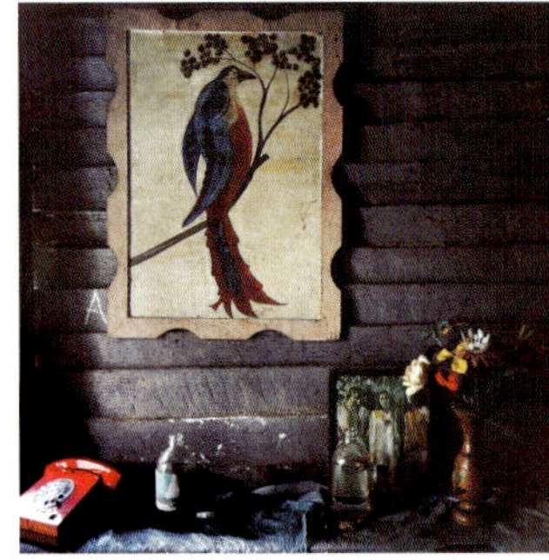

Baracoa, Guantanamo, July 2001

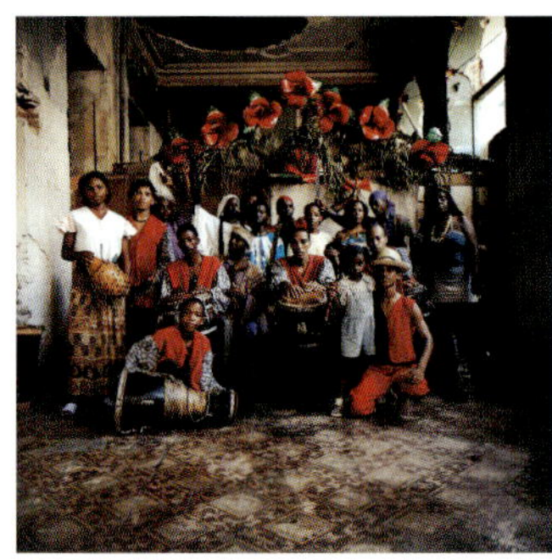

Folk group Icatce, Santiago de Cuba, May 2002

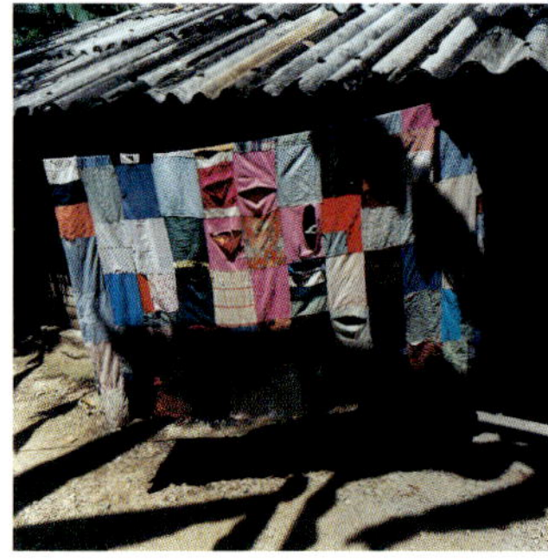

Baracoa, Guantanamo, July 2002

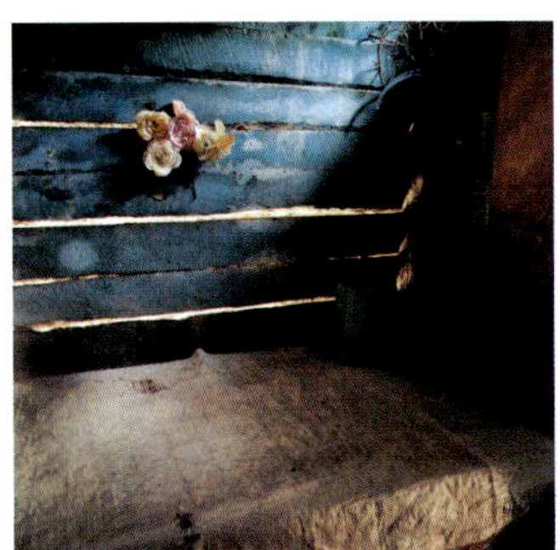

Baracoa, Guantanamo, June 2002

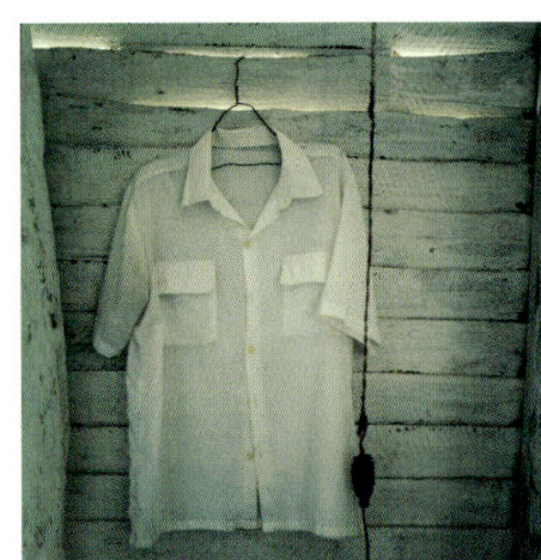

Vinales, Pinal del Rio, May 2002

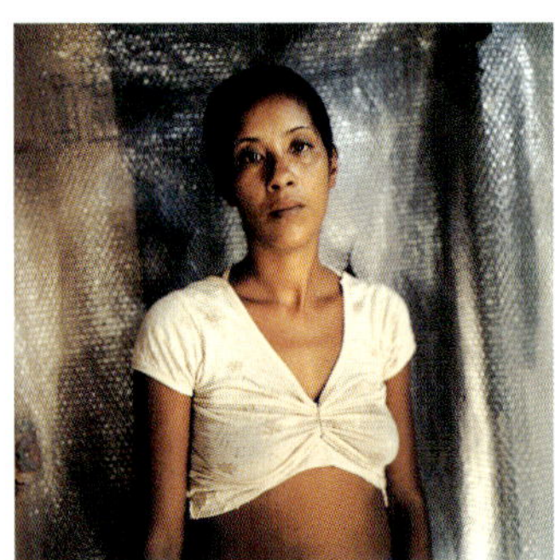

Odilis Romero, Desi, Santiago de Cuba, July 2001

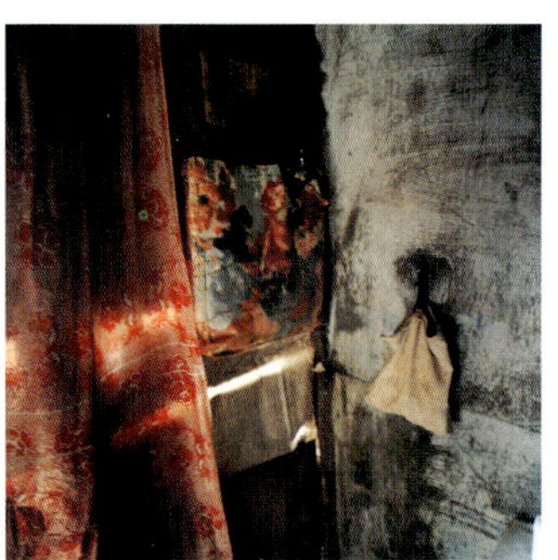

Baracoa, Guantanamo, July 2001

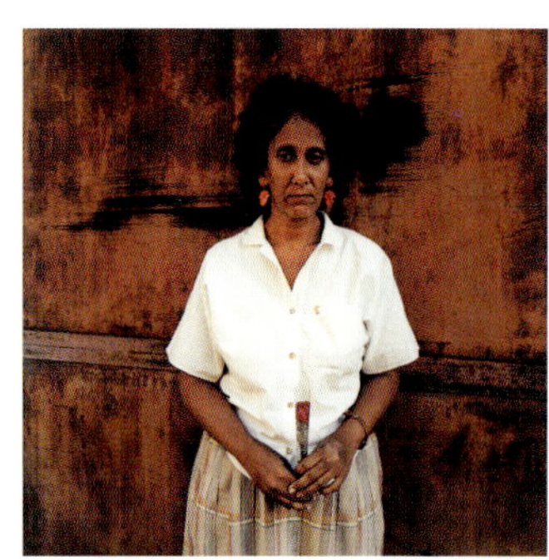

Ines Maria, Santiago de Cuba, June 2001

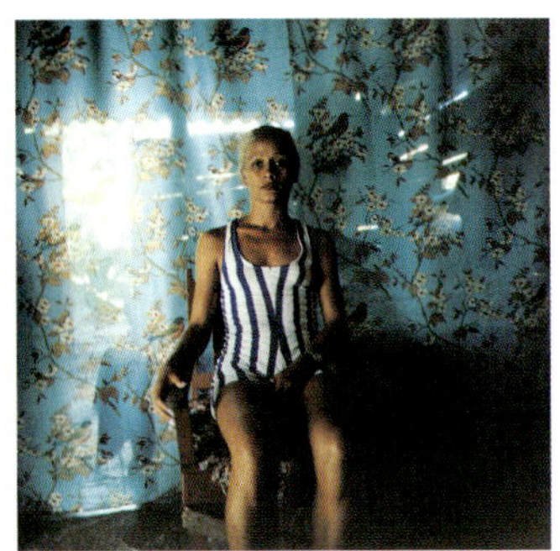

Kenia Machado, Baracoa, May 2002

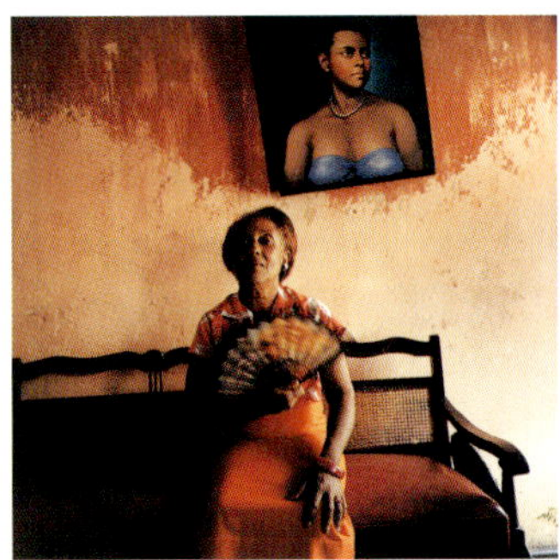

Jojefina, Santiago de Cuba, June 2001

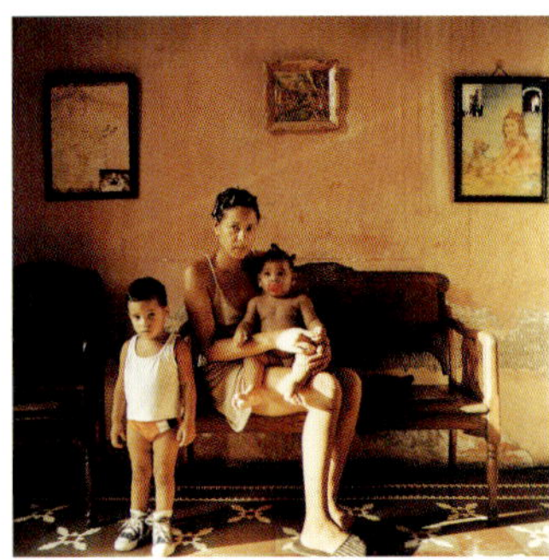

Anna Rosa and kids, Municipal, Santiago de Cuba, April 2002

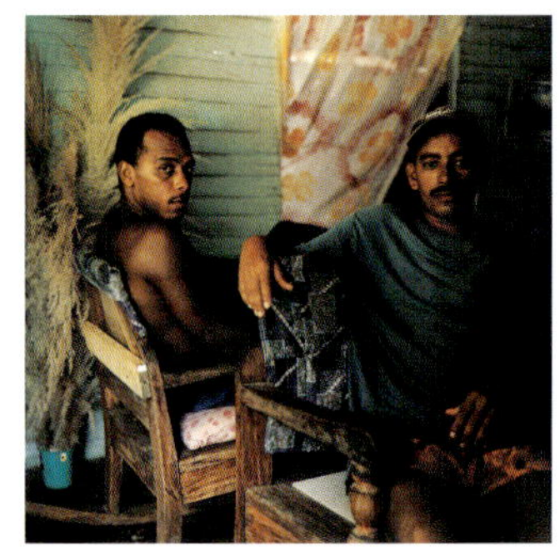

David and his friend, Baracoa, Guantanamo, June 2002

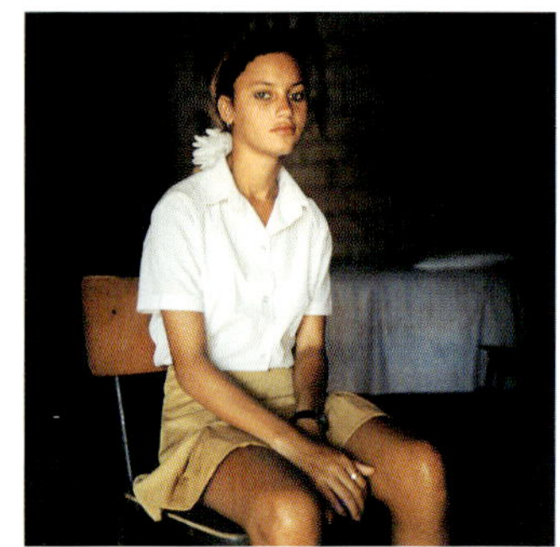

Lasara Placere, Trinidad, Sancti Spiritus, May 2002

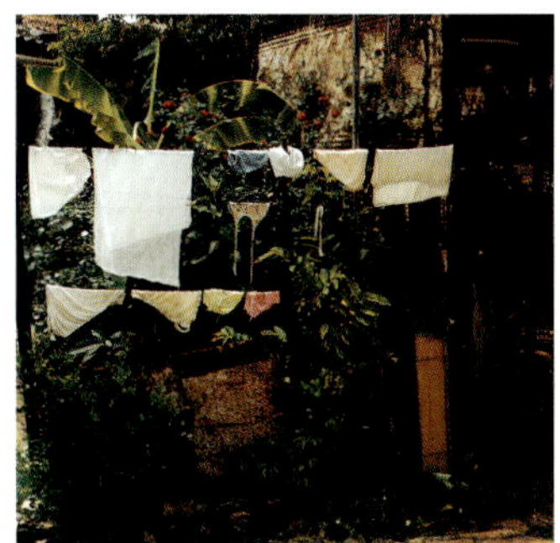

Trinidad, Sancti Spiritus, June 2002

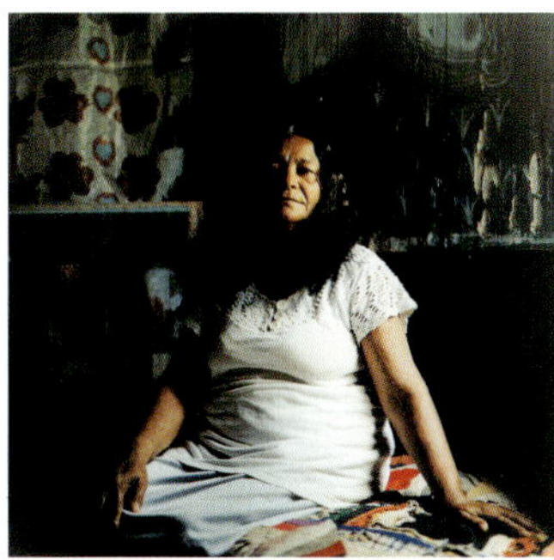

Gladis Duran Ramirez, Baracoa, Guantanamo, May 2002

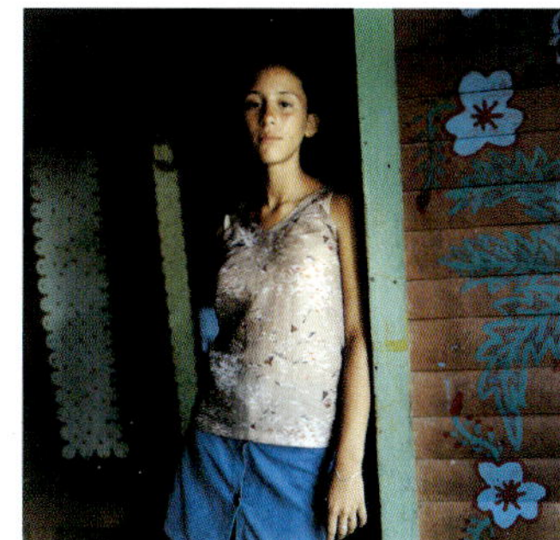

Yarisladis Dias Cala, Baracoa, Guantanamo, May 2002

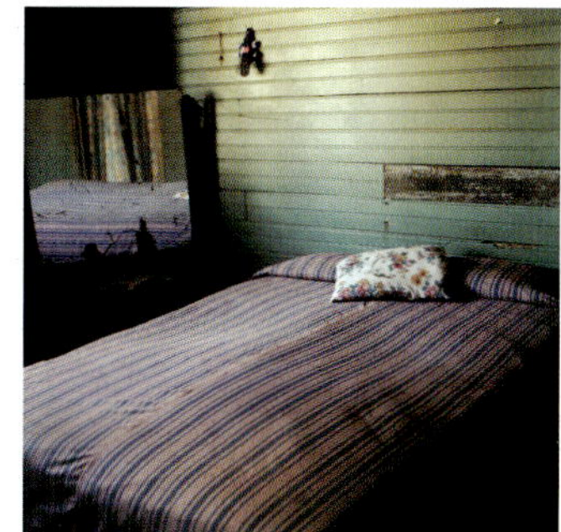

Trinidad, Sancti Spiritus, June 2001

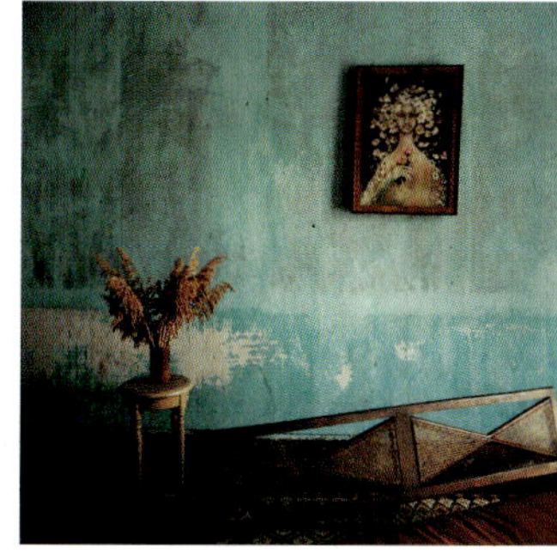

Manzanillo, Granma, June 2002

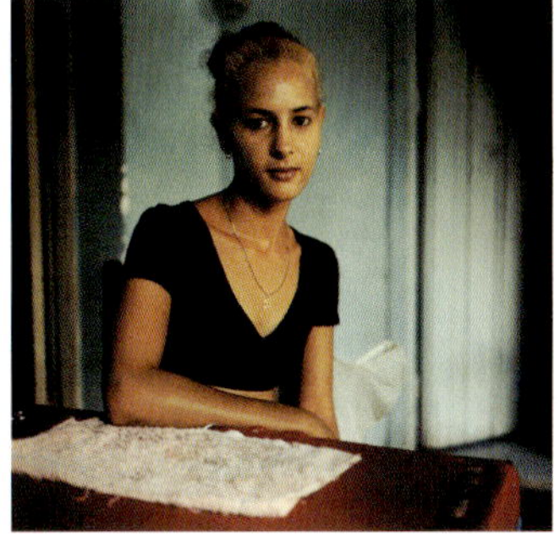

Marreli, Las Tunas, May 2002

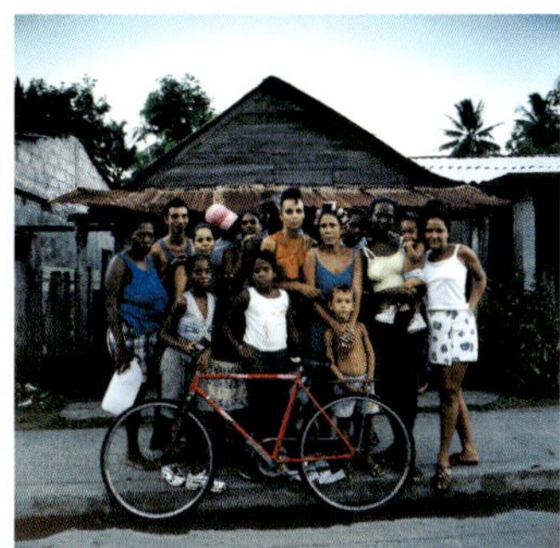

Baracoa, Guantanamo, July 2001

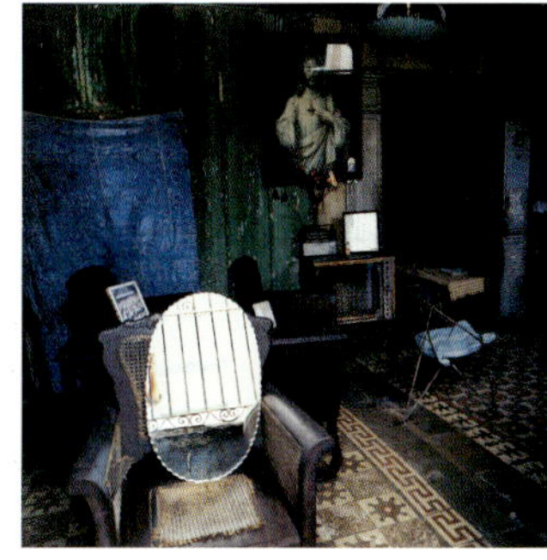

El Tivoli, Santiago de Cuba, June 2002

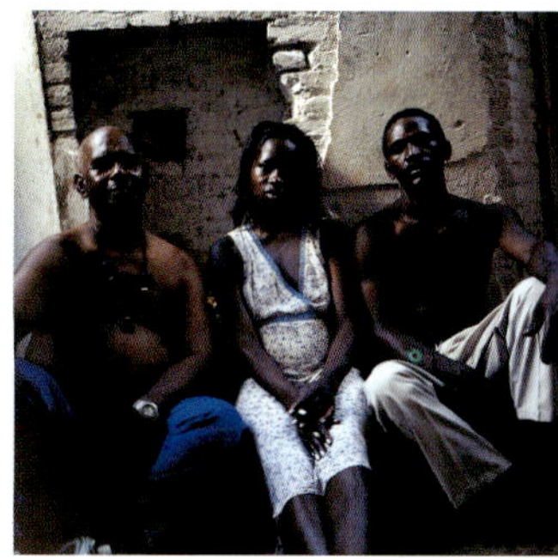

Rojelia and her friends, Santiago de Cuba, June 2002

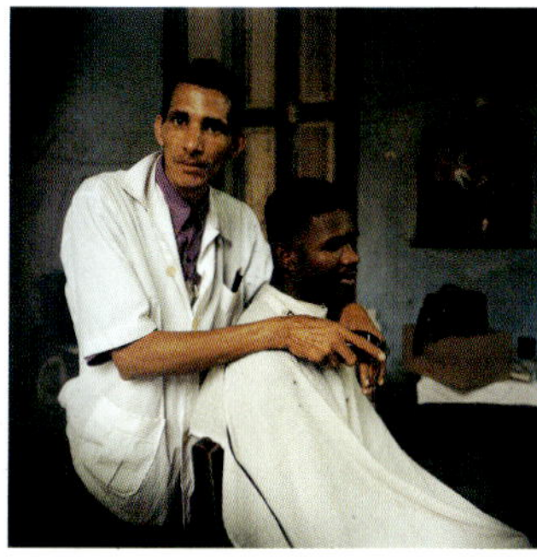

German Pozo Baldes and his friend, Centro Havana, Havana, May 2002

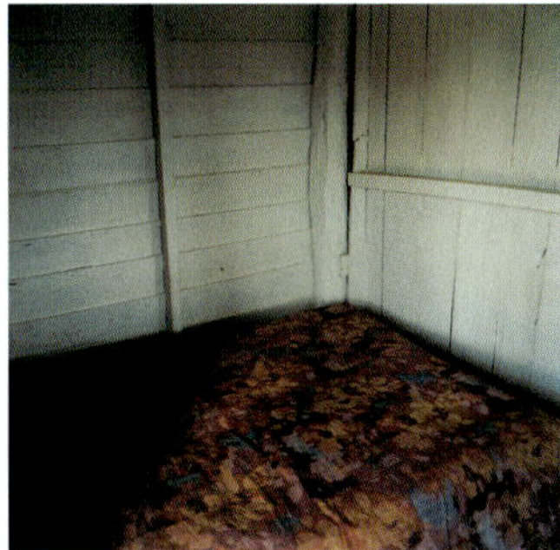

Remedios, Santa Clara, June 2001

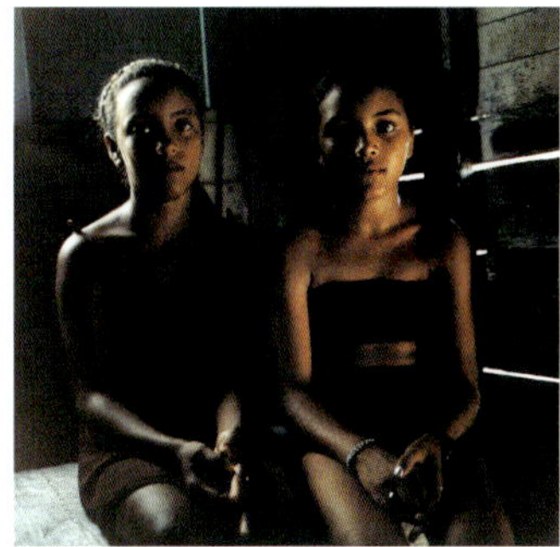

Lucia and Anna, Pesceda, Granma, May 2002

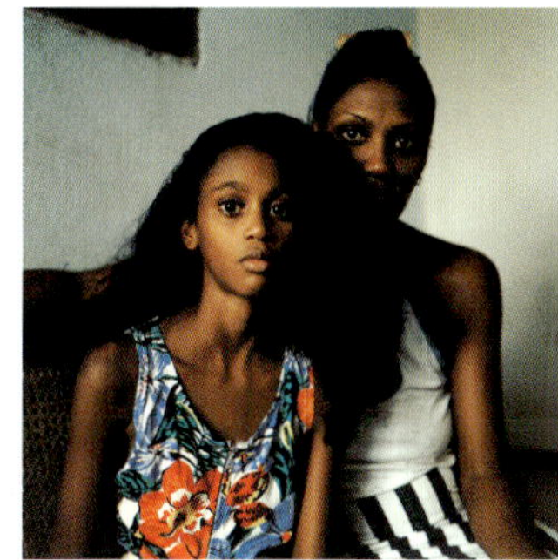

Eliersis Torres Morales and her mother, Municipal, Santiago de Cuba, May 2002

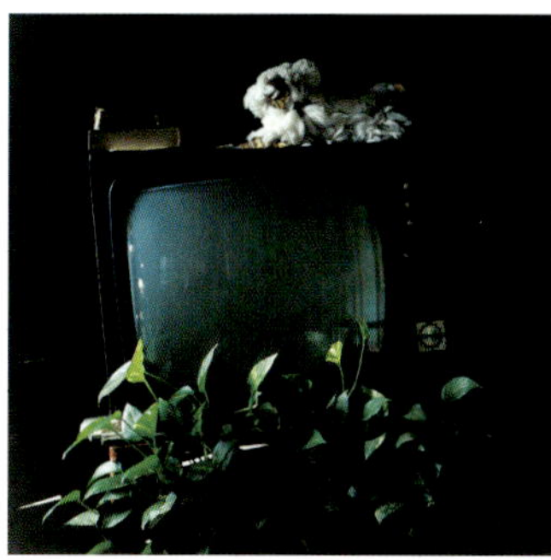

Maisi, Guantanamo, June 2002

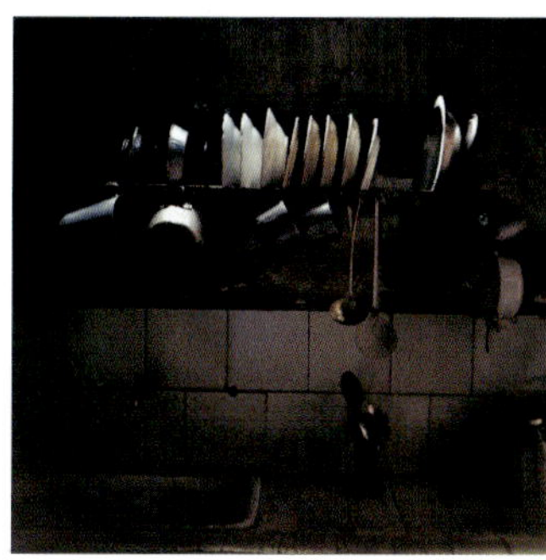

Manzanillo, Granma, July 2001

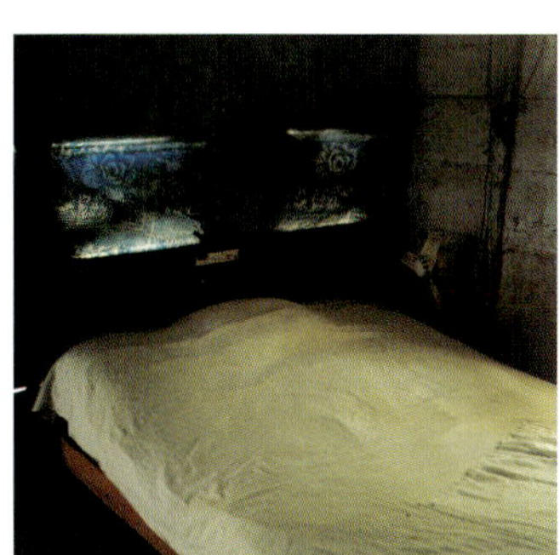

Baracoa, Guantanamo, June 2001

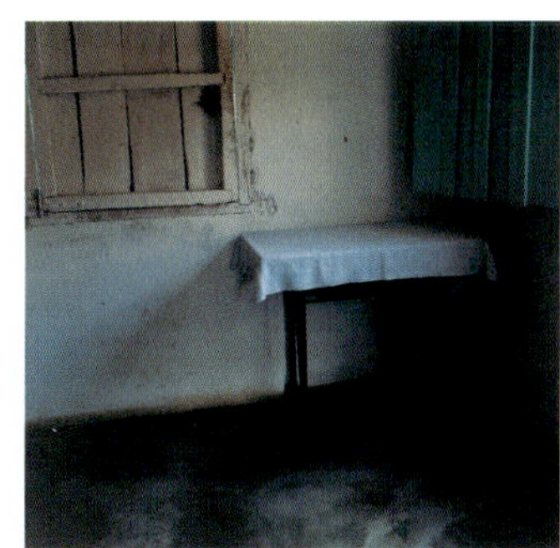

Vinales, Pinal del Rio, May 2002

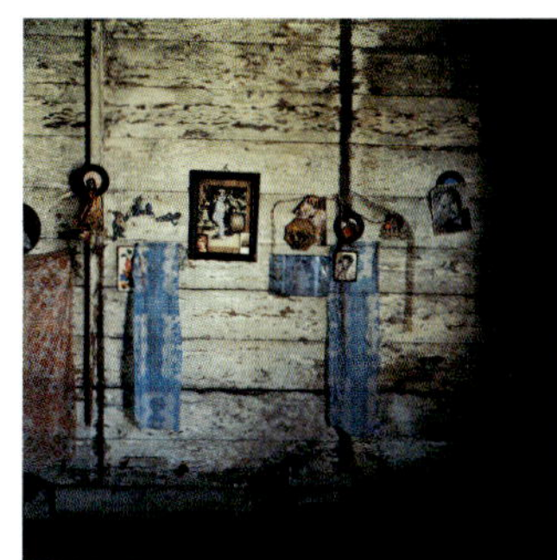

Manzanillo, Granma, June 2002

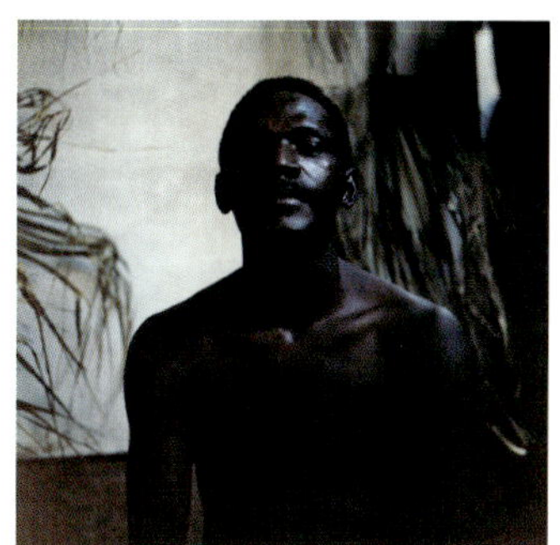

Ramon, Santiago de Cuba, June 2002

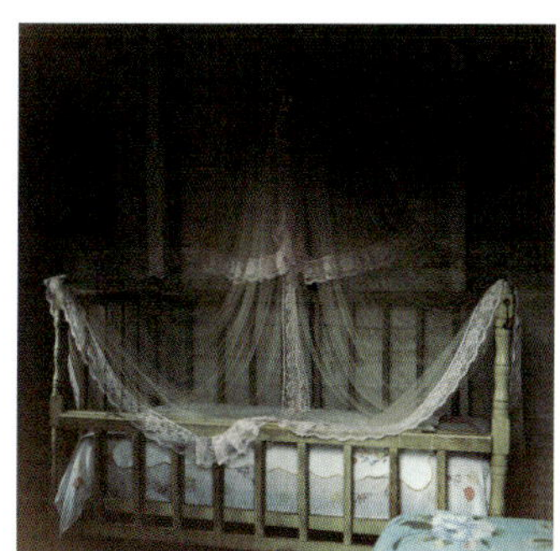

Vinales, Pinal del Rio, May 2002

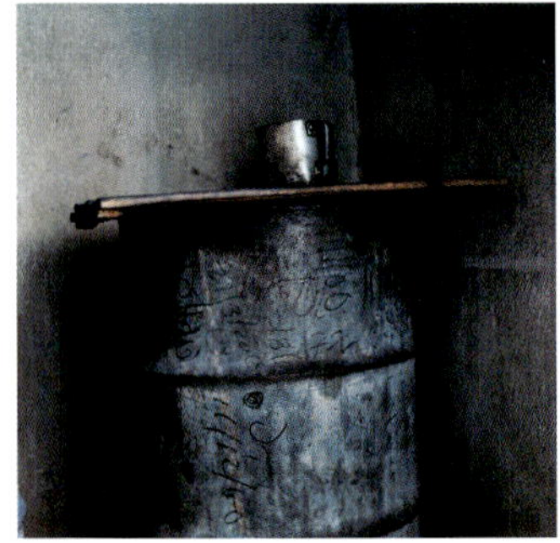

El Tivoli, Santiago de Cuba,
June 2001

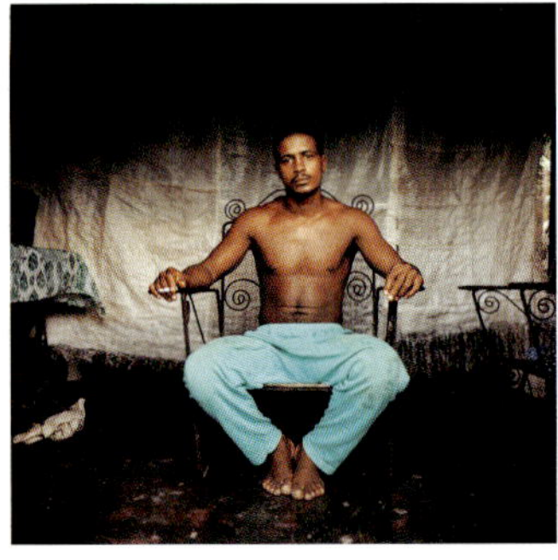

Miguel, Baracoa, Guantanamo,
May 2002

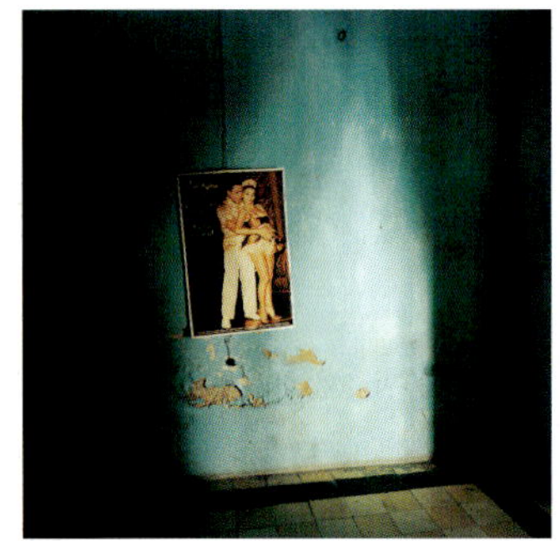

Bayamo, Granma, July 2001

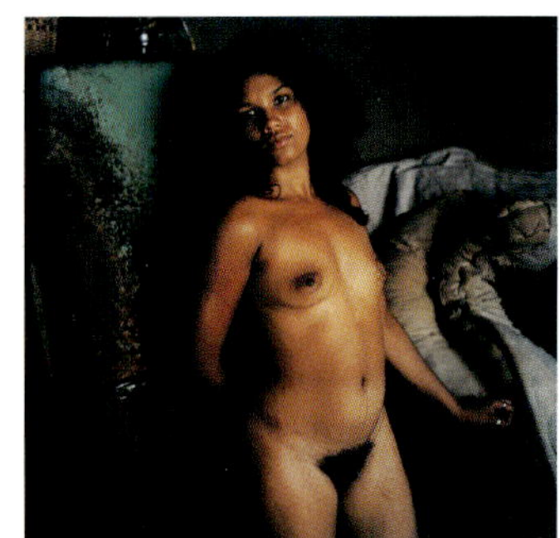

Dayisel, Santiago de Cuba,
May 2002

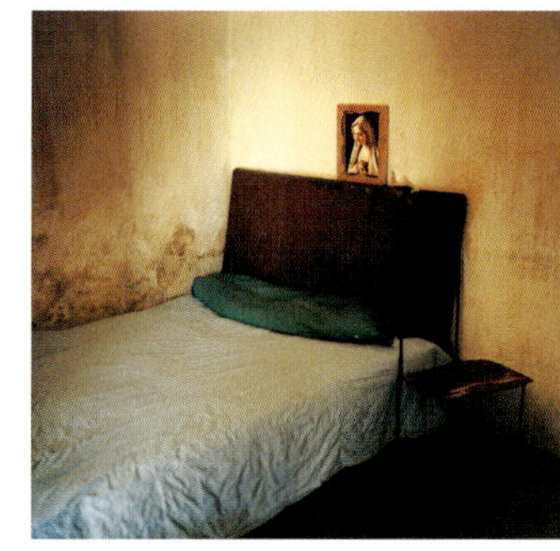

Trinidad, Sancti Spiritus,
June 2002

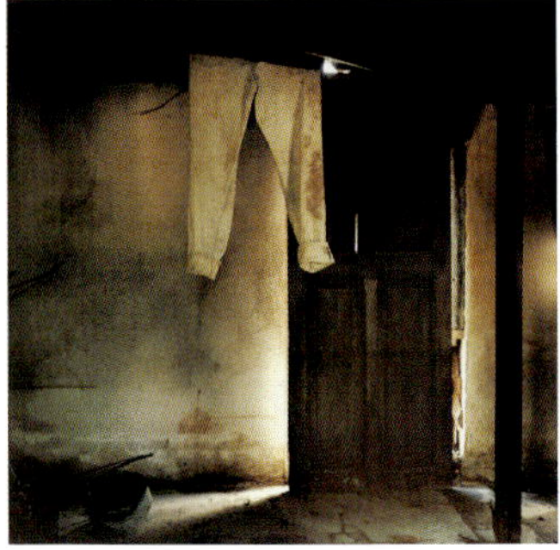

Havana, July 2001

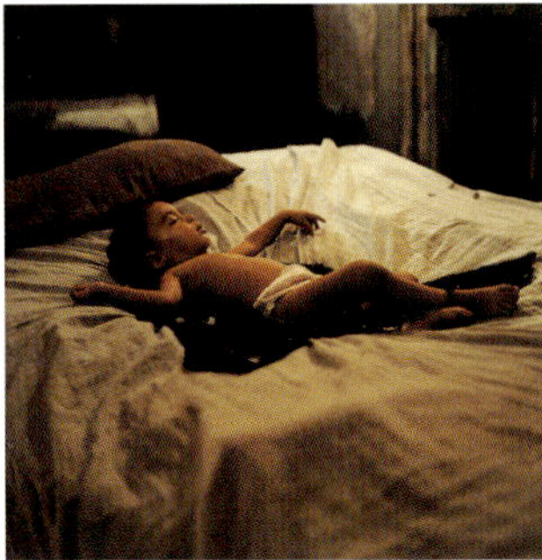

Nina, Manzanillo, Granma,
April 2002

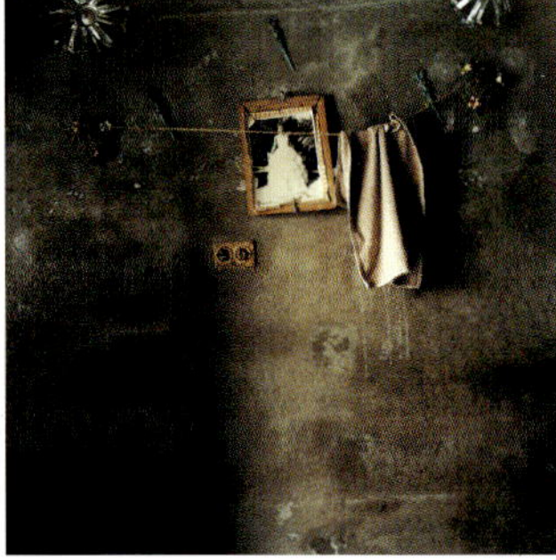

Manzanillo, Granma, May 2002

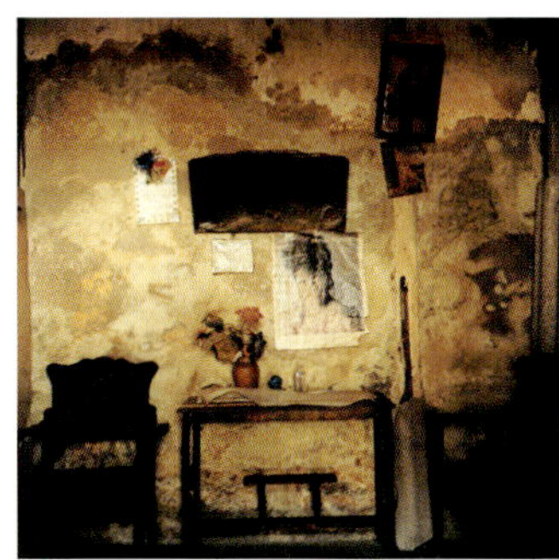

Los Olmos, Santiago de Cuba,
July 2001

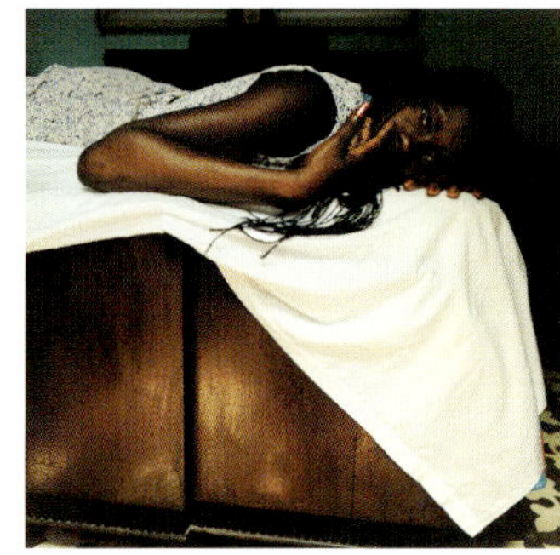

Rojelia Concebo, El Tivoli,
Santiago de Cuba, June 2002

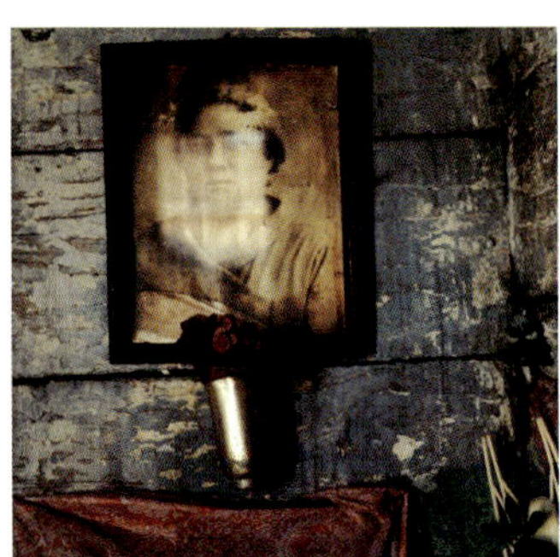

Vinales, Pinal del Rio, May 2002

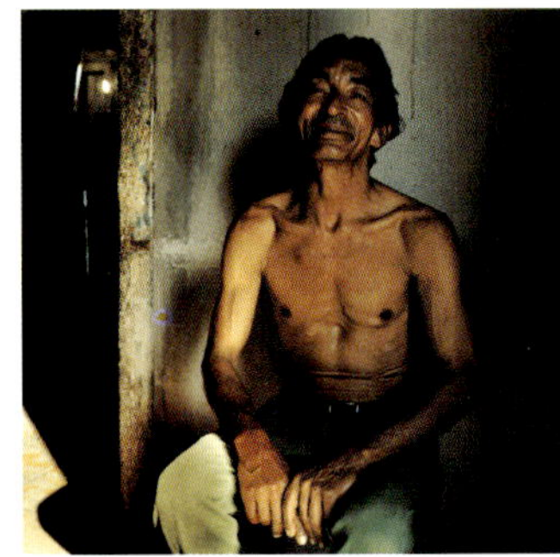

Juan, Manzanillo, Granma,
June 2002

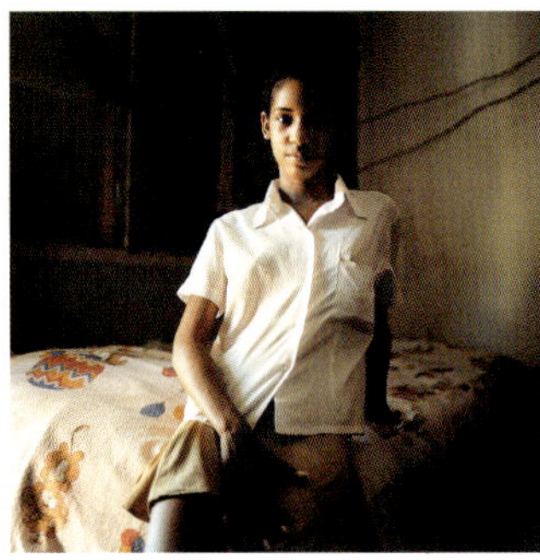

Elizabeth, Trocha, Santiago de Cuba,
June 2001

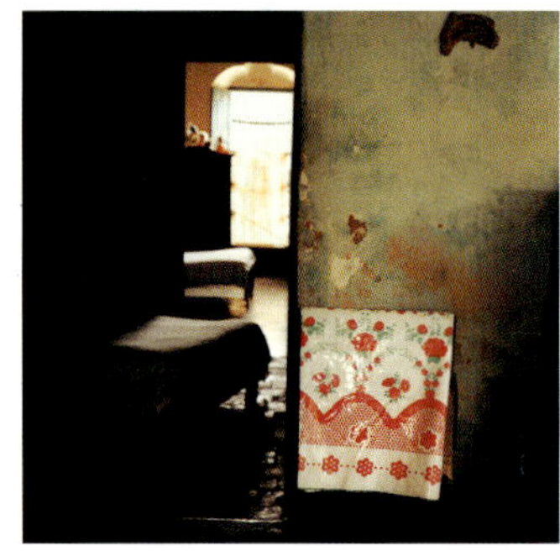

Trinidad, Sancti Spiritus, July 2002

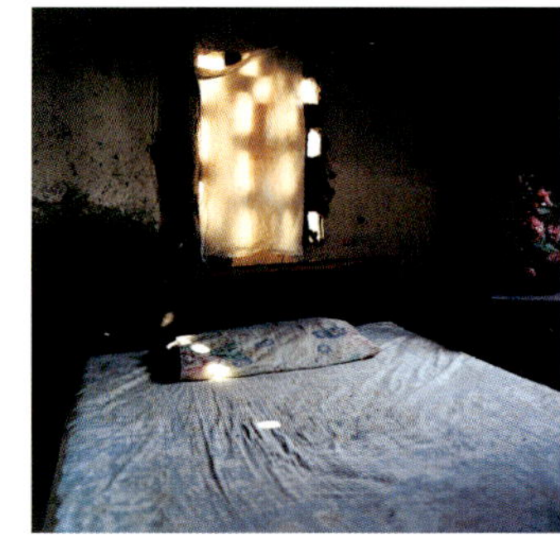

Bayamo, Granma, July 2001

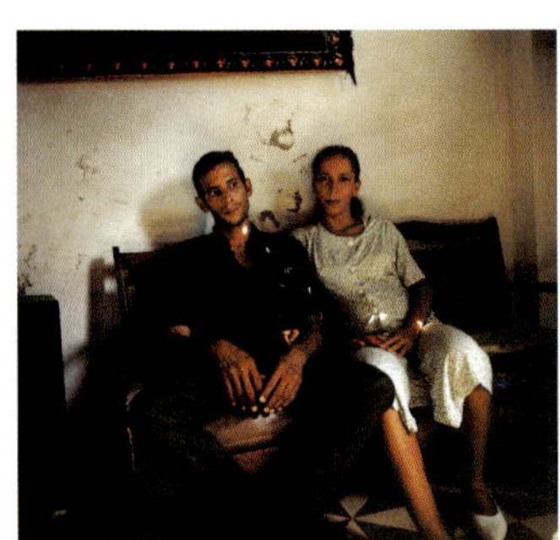

Mayra and Lazaro, Tsitsarones,
Santiago de Cuba, May 2002

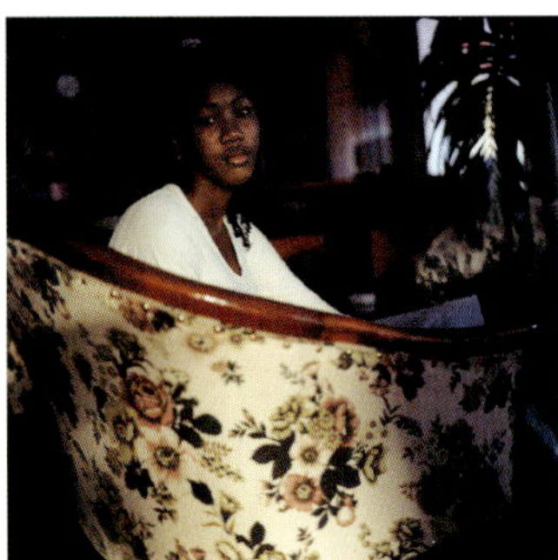

Yaimi Kindelan, Santiago de Cuba,
June 2002

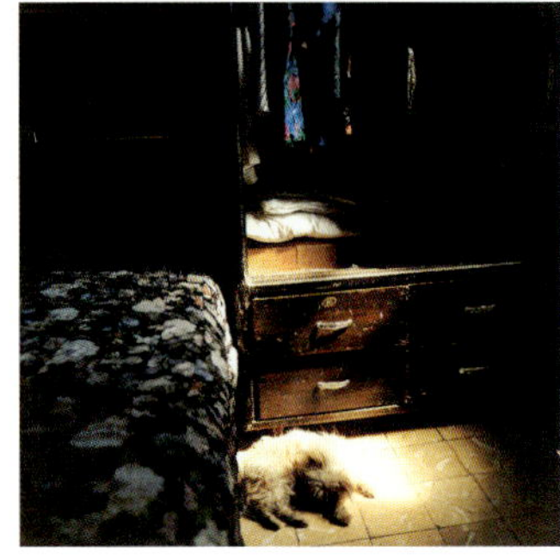

Guanabacoa, Havana, May 2002

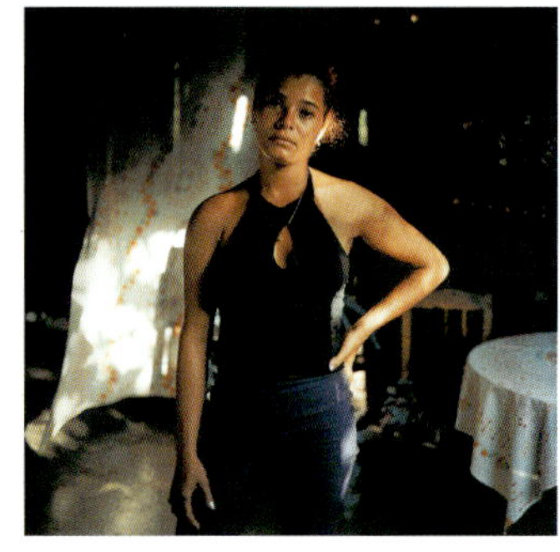

Diosalin, Baracoa, Guantanamo,
April 2002

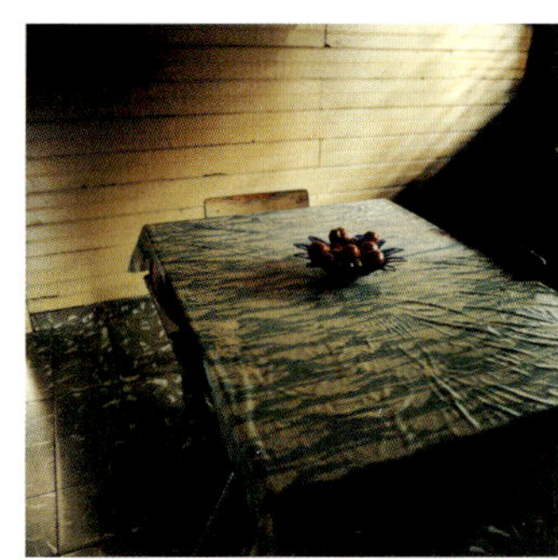

Tsitsarones, Santiago de Cuba,
July 2002

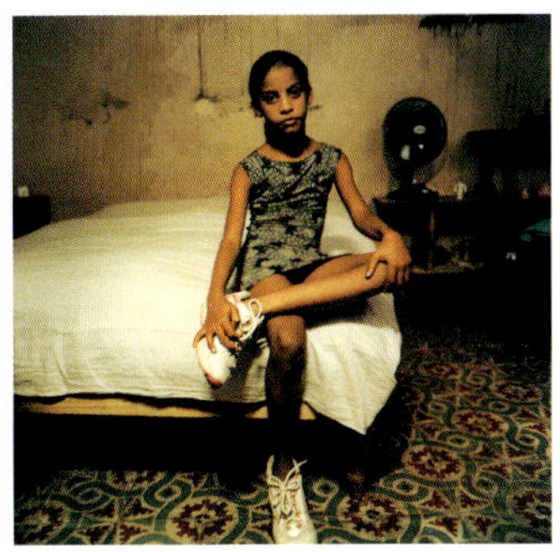

Rafaela, Havana Vieja, Havana, June 2001

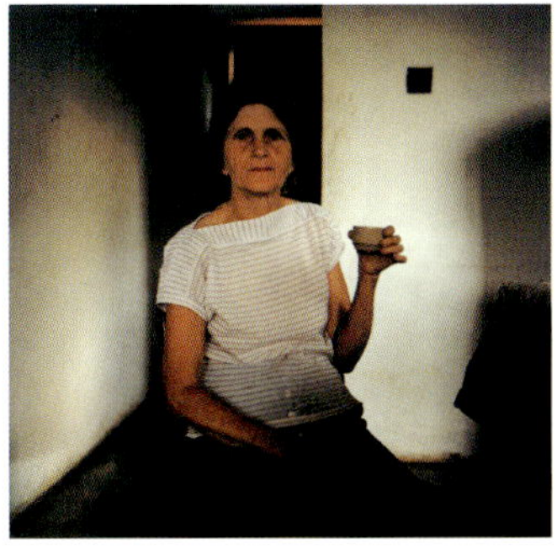

Mariana, Vinales, Pinal del Rio, May 2002

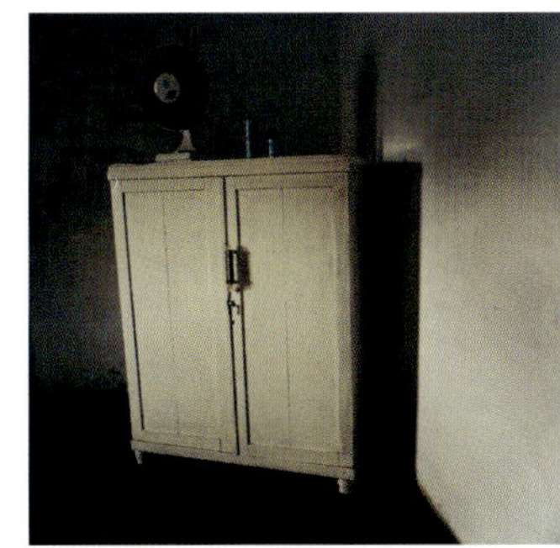

Pesceda, Granma, May 2002

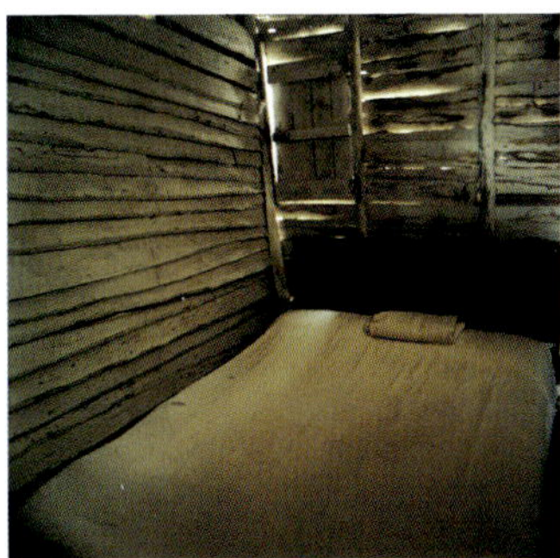

Vinales, Pinal del Rio, May 2002

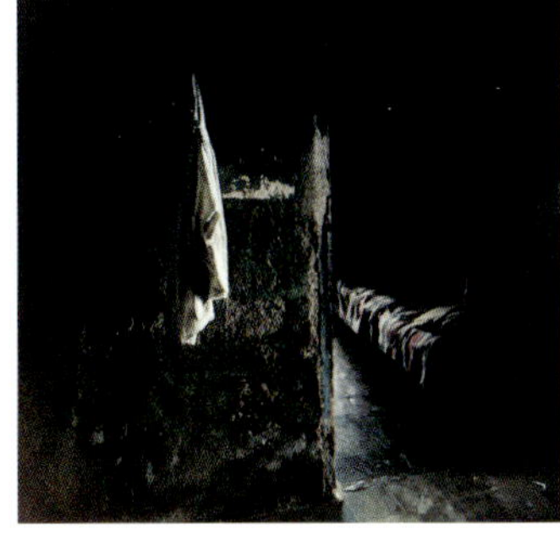

Manzanillo, Granma, June 2002

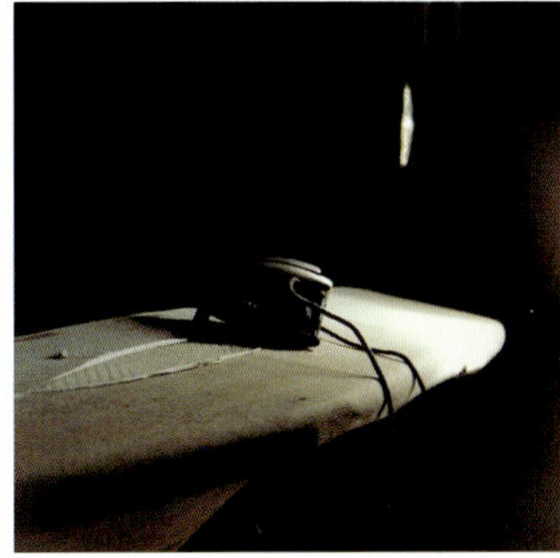

Guanabacoa, Havana, June 2001

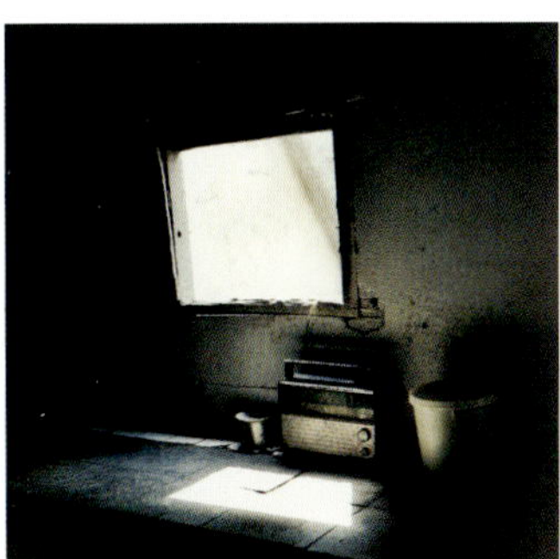

Remedios, Santa Clara, May 2002

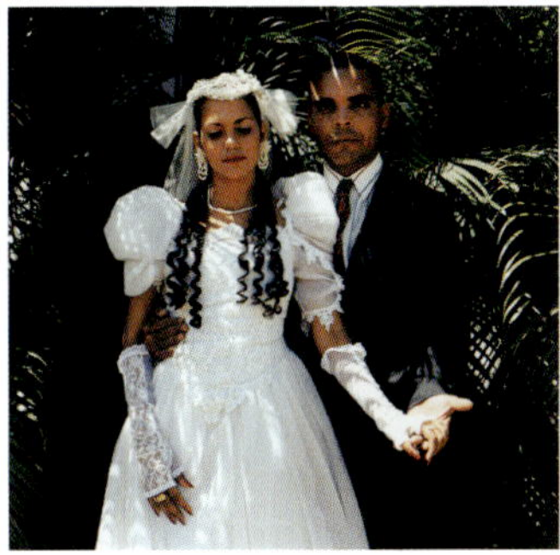

Michel Zeira and Claudia Maydol, Manzanillo, Granma, June 2002

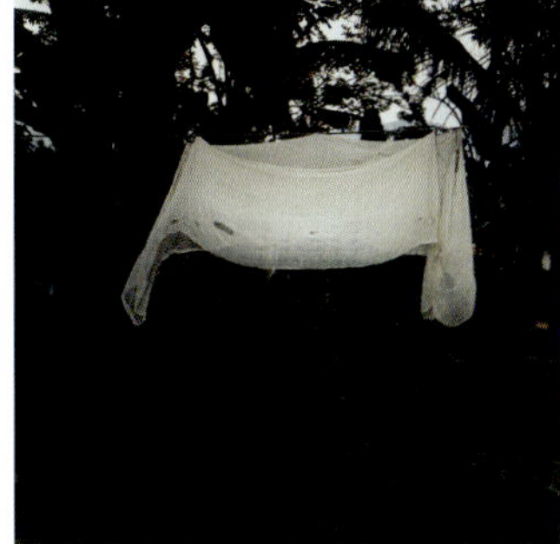

Trinidad, Sancti Spiritus, June 2002

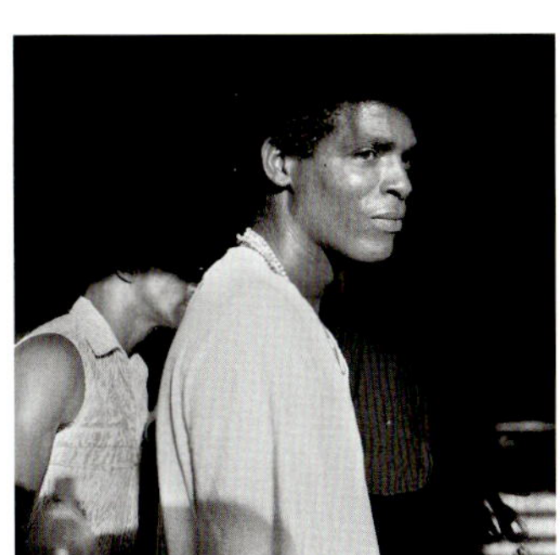

Felippe, Los Olmos, Santiago de Cuba, July 2001

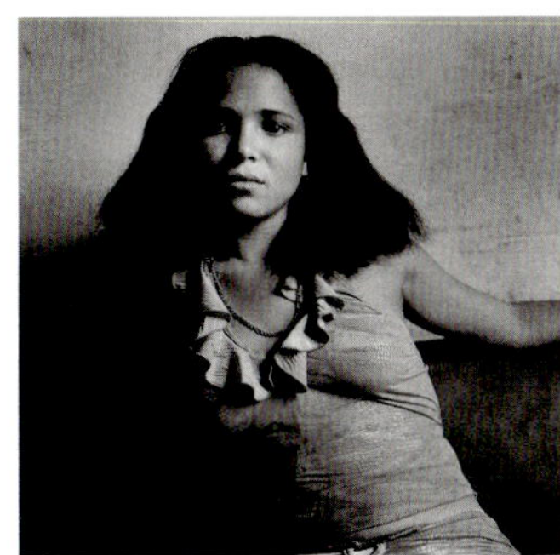

Juliana, Santiago de Cuba, July 2001

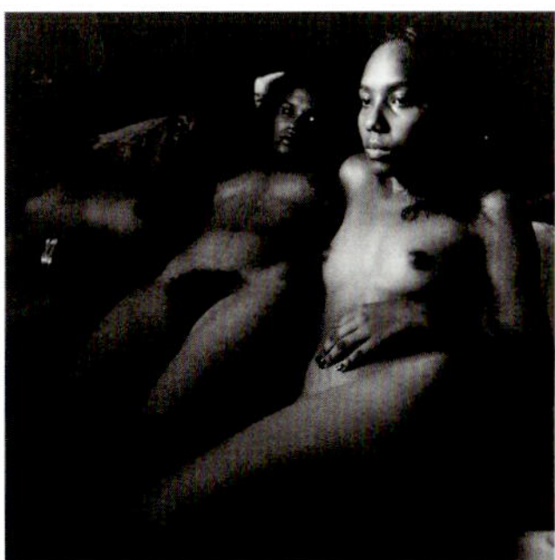

Yaneisis and Dayisel, Santiago de Cuba, June 2002

European Publishers Award
for Photography 2003
tenth edition

Jury

Jean Paul Capitani
Actes Sud

John Demos
Apeiron Photos

Dewi Lewis
Dewi Lewis Publishing

Jonas Braus
Edition Braus

Andrés Gamboa
Lunwerg Editores

Mario Peliti
Peliti Associati

Jean-Luc Monterosso
Maison Européenne de la Photographie

Gero Furchheim
Leica Camera AG

In collaboration with

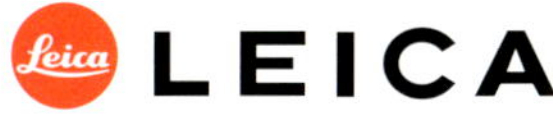